Lecture Notes in Computer Science   10788

Commenced Publication in 1973
Founding and Former Series Editors:
Gerhard Goos, Juris Hartmanis, and Jan van Leeuwen

More information about this series at http://www.springer.com/series/7407

Meng Wang · Scott Owens (Eds.)

Trends in Functional Programming

18th International Symposium, TFP 2017
Canterbury, UK, June 19–21, 2017
Revised Selected Papers

Springer

Editors
Meng Wang
University of Bristol
Bristol
UK

Scott Owens
University of Kent
Kent
UK

ISSN 0302-9743 ISSN 1611-3349 (electronic)
Lecture Notes in Computer Science
ISBN 978-3-319-89718-9 ISBN 978-3-319-89719-6 (eBook)
https://doi.org/10.1007/978-3-319-89719-6

Library of Congress Control Number: 2018940147

LNCS Sublibrary: SL1 – Theoretical Computer Science and General Issues

Printed on acid-free paper

This Springer imprint is published by the registered company Springer International Publishing AG part of Springer Nature
The registered company address is: Gewerbestrasse 11, 6330 Cham, Switzerland

Preface

This volume contains a selection of the papers presented at TFP 2017: the Symposium on Trends in Function Programming 2017, held during June 19–21, 2017, in Canterbury, UK.

TFP is an international forum for researchers with interests in all aspects of functional programming, taking a broad view of current and future trends in the area. It aspires to be a lively environment for presenting the latest research results and other contributions, described in draft papers submitted prior to the symposium. For the symposium, the Program Committee chair verified that these drafts were within the scope of TFP. Submissions appearing in the draft proceedings are not considered as peer-reviewed publications.

The TFP 2017 program consisted of two invited talks and 21 presentations. The invited talks were given by Conor McBride (University of Strathclyde, UK) on "Everybody's Got to be Somewhere," and Cătălin Hrițcu (Inria Paris, France) on "Verified Effectful Programming in F*." The 21 presentations led to a total of 16 full papers submitted to the formal post-refereeing process. Each submission was reviewed by at least three reviewers. The Program Committee selected eight papers, which are included in these proceedings.

We are grateful to everyone at the University of Kent for their help in preparing and organizing TFP 2017, in particular Olaf Chitil and Jo Sharrad. We also gratefully acknowledge the assistance of the TFP 2017 Program Committee and the TFP Steering Committee for their advice while organizing the symposium.

February 2018

Meng Wang
Scott Owens

Organization

Program Co-chairs

Meng Wang   University of Bristol, UK
Scott Owens   University of Kent, UK

Program Committee

Jeremy Yallop   University of Cambridge, UK
Nicolas Wu   University of Bristol, UK
Laura Castro   University of A Coruña, Spain
Gabriel Scherer   Northeastern University, USA
Edwin Brady   University of St. Andrews, UK
Janis Voigtländer   Radboud University Nijmegen, The Netherlands
Peter Achten   Radboud University Nijmegen, The Netherlands
Tom Schrijvers   KU Leuven, Belgium
Matthew Fluet   Rochester Institute of Technology, USA
Mauro Jaskelioff   CIFASIS/Universidad Nacional de Rosario, Argentina
Patricia Johann   Appalachian State University, USA
Bruno Oliveira   The University of Hong Kong, SAR China
Rita Loogen   Philipps-Universität Marburg, Germany
David Van Horn   University of Maryland, USA
Soichiro Hidaka   Hosei University, Japan
Michał Pałka   Chalmers University of Technology, Sweden
Sandrine Blazy   University of Rennes 1 – IRISA, France

Additional Reviewers

Reuben Rowe   University of Kent, UK
Pablo Lamela-Seijas   University of Kent, UK

Contents

Memoized Flat Closures for CPS
or Taming Memory Allocation for λ in CPS

Marco T. Morazán[1]($\boxtimes$), Lindsey M. Reams[2], Nicholas R. Olson[1],
and Shamil Dzhatdoyev[1]

[1] Seton Hall University, South Orange, USA
{morazanm,dzhatdsh}@shu.edu, nrolson5@gmail.com
[2] University of Massachusetts, Lowell, USA
reamslin@gmail.com

Abstract. Compilers for functional languages are judged, in part, on
how well they handle λ-expressions. The evaluation of λ-expressions tra-
ditionally requires closure allocations which can be intensive and can
interact poorly with a garbage collector. Work on closure representation and garbage collection has successfully improved this interaction.
This work, however, does not address the actual allocation of closures in
the first place. This is important, because the only closures that do not
have to be garbage collected are the closures that are never allocated.
This article explores a novel mechanism to reduce flat-closure allocations based on memoization. To test this new mechanism, a compiler
has been developed that uses continuation-passing style as an intermediate representation–which makes closure allocation ubiquitous. Empirical
results strongly suggest that flat-closure memoization is an important
optimization that significantly reduces running time as well as memory
and closure allocation.

1 Introduction

Functional languages have a reputation for heavy memory allocation. Heavy
memory allocation on modern computer architectures is a problem that limits
performance given that CPU speeds are much faster than memory speeds [1].
To mitigate the problem of heavy memory allocation (and to liberate programmers from low-level memory management), virtually all functional languages are
garbage collected. Garbage collection automatically recycles memory occupied
by data that is no longer in use by a program [2]. Although garbage collection
makes programs easier to write and maintain, it does not keep memory allocation and occupation minimal [3]. In fact, it has been empirically demonstrated
that conservative garbage collection algorithms significantly decrease locality of
reference causing one or two orders of magnitude more page faults [4][1]. Thus,
it is desirable for programming languages to minimize memory allocation and,
therefore, spark fewer garbage collections.

---

[1] This study, however, was performed using the imperative C language.

© Springer International Publishing AG, part of Springer Nature 2018
M. Wang and S. Owens (Eds.): TFP 2017, LNCS 10788, pp. 1–18, 2018.
https://doi.org/10.1007/978-3-319-89719-6_1

A feature of functional languages that allocates memory is the implementation of first-class functions. To represent a function at runtime, functional languages allocate a closure–a data structure that stores the bindings of free variables and (a pointer to) the body of the function to be evaluated, if at all, in the future of the computation. Early implementations of functional languages, like Henderson's Lisp [5] using a SECD machine [6], used linked closures (a.k.a deep closures). This closure representation makes closure creation fast at the expense of making the resolution of variable references slower [7]. In addition, bindings that are no longer relevant to a computation are unnecessarily kept alive (i.e., not garbage collected) by storing all lexically defined variables as part of the closure. To make accesses to free variables faster and to make garbage collection more effective, many functional languages use flat closures [8] (a.k.a display closures [7]). These advantages come at the cost of making closure creation slower as the bindings of free variables must be copied to the closure. If free variable accesses are more frequent than closure creation, then the extra cost of closure creation is amortized over such accesses and over less garbage collection. To reduce the copying of bindings done to create flat closures, safely-linked closures allow for bindings to be shared between closures [9]. This closure representation makes closure creation faster than flat-closure creation at the expense of adding overhead to the resolution of references to free variables. Unlike linked closures, bindings are only kept alive while they may still be relevant to the computation allowing the memory space they occupy to be recycled as soon as possible by a garbage collector.

The work done on closure representation successfully addresses interfacing with a garbage collector to efficiently reclaim memory. It does not, however, address how to avoid closure allocations in the first place. The relationship between safely-linked closures and flat closures, however, suggests a new mechanism for reducing closure allocation. In essence, this relationship is based on the similarity of different closures. This similarity stems from the fact that closures may store some or all of the same values. These similarities can be memoized and, thus, allocated once and reused many times to reduce memory allocation. For instance, consider the following code to compute the operands of a function application in a typical interpreter:

```
; (listof expr) environment --> (listof expr-vals)
(define (eval-operands rands env)
  (map (lambda (e) (eval-expr e env)) rands))
```

Evaluating the expression

```
(f (h ...) (g ...) (f ...))
```

leads to (at least) four calls to eval-operands. Each of these calls evaluates the lambda expression to create a single-value closure with the same binding for env. Instead of allocating the same closure four times, the closure can be allocated once for the outer call to f, memoized, and reused for the calls to h, g, and the inner call to f.

This article explores the impact memoizing flat closures has on memory allocation and on running time using the Green programming language. To effectively explore this impact, Green uses continuation-passing style (CPS) as an intermediate representation to make the use of closures ubiquitous. Section 2 briefly discusses related work and draws contrasts with the work presented in this article. Section 3 describes two strategies to memoize flat closures. It outlines how to capture the repetition in closure creation that makes memoization effective. The key to success is to implement closures for user-defined functions differently than closures for continuations. Section 4 briefly describes the Green programming language and the Green Virtual Machine (GVM). Section 5 presents empirical results. Finally, Sect. 6 presents concluding remarks and future work.

2   Related Work

There is a long history in compilers for functional languages that discusses how to allocate closures. In fact, historically many compilers treat closures for continuations differently than closures for user-defined functions. The driving force behind this is that the success of compilers, in part, depends on their ability to handle λ-expressions [10]. The RABBIT compiler, for example, makes a distinction between λ-expressions and continuations, and between function calls and continuation invocations, to facilitate code generation [11]. For user-defined function calls, code for argument set-up is followed by code for the body of a λ. In the case of a continuation, a function is first called placing its value in an appropriate place to then call the continuation. In contrast, Green treats function and continuation applications in the same general manner: register set-up followed by a call. Nonetheless, Green also treats continuations differently by making them implicit parameters to user-defined functions much like the heap is an implicit parameter. Another difference between Green and RABBIT is that RABBIT adds continuations to primitive functions which is not done in Green.

The Orbit compiler reduces the amount of memory used by closures by determining when a closure can be allocated on a stack (or in registers) instead of the heap [12]. In addition, Orbit packs code pointers that reference the same variables into a single runtime structure. This means that closures share values (like safely-linked closures) and are allocated as soon as the bindings of the free variables are known. Closures are heap-allocated when they are used as a non-continuation argument. Continuation-closures are allocated on a stack given that they are used once and never used again. The work done with Green reveals, in contrast, that if continuation-closures are heap-allocated, so that they can be memoized, then this can lead to speed-ups. However, continuation-closures are so short lived and reused relatively little that not heap allocating them (and only memoizing noncontinuation-closures) leads to consistently larger speed-ups. In addition, continuation-closures are stored in an accumulator akin to Orbit's strategy to stack continuations. In fact, a stack is one implementation strategy for an accumulator that follows a last-in first-out access pattern–precisely how continuations are accessed.

The Pascal compiler also treats continuation-closures differently [13]. Like Orbit, continuation-closures are stack-allocated. Non-continuation-closures are also stack-allocated when it can be proven that when invoking its control context (i.e., the current continuation) the function cannot be called again. In contrast to compilers that stack-allocate continuations and never use them again once popped off the stack, the re-use of these closures avoids a significant amount of memory allocation through memoization. That is, Green debunks the common belief that continuation-closures must only be used once to achieve speed-ups and better memory utilization. The key to success in Green is to not store continuations as a part of any closure. Despite the gains observed by memoizing continuations, the empirical data in this article, however, also strongly suggests that even larger speed-ups are obtained by a CPS-based compiler when continuations are stacked and not memoized.

The SML/NJ compiler does not stack-allocate continuation-closures [14]. Instead, all closures are heap-allocated. The reasoning behind this implementation choice is that garbage collection need not be expensive and, therefore, the expected difference in performance is not large. In contrast, the work presented here explores both the stacking of heap-allocated continuations and of non-heap-allocated continuations. The continuation accumulator in Green allows for control to be an implicit argument to functions. Heap allocation of closures, of course, ought to only be done if it leads to the best speed-ups when using memoization.

The debate over compiling with or without continuations rages on. Detractors of CPS favor using A-normal form (ANF) as an intermediate representation [15,16]. They argue that an ANF-based compiler can do just as naturally almost anything that is done by a CPS-based compiler. One important exception, however, is converting calls to known functions into jumps. Given that continuations are not explicit in ANF, it is difficult to naturally perform this optimization. Other detractors of CPS point out that CPS terms are complex and that it is costly to allocate closures for the λ-expressions introduced by the transformation. These drawbacks, however, are considered more apparent than real by some as efficient code can be generated from a CPS representation [17]. Furthermore, it is argued that inlining is simpler in a CPS representation. The work presented in this article does not resolve the CPS versus ANF (versus contification [18]) debate, but does strongly suggest that there is value in closure memoization. Even if λ-expressions are less common in ANF-based and contification-based compilers, the data presented in this article shows significant speed-ups and significant less memory allocation for noncontinuation-closures when memoization is used. The benefits are greater when only noncontinuation-closures are memoized and continuation-closures are not heap-allocated. Furthermore, the work presented suggests that the penalty incurred to allocate closures for continuations introduced by the CPS transformation is not as severe as commonly believed if memoization is utilized.

3   Closure Memoization

Memoization requires carefully addressing equality and caching with precise dependencies [19]. Equality in the context of closure memoization refers to being able to determine if a closure is cached. Determining closure equality is achieved by exploiting the naming convention used for closures. Each memoized closure is given a fresh identifier that is a linear combination of the heap addresses of the bindings of the free variables and the address of the code to be evaluated. Caching with precise dependencies in this context refers to storing closures with respect to the bindings of the free variables and the code to be executed. The naming strategy described guarantees that closures are cached with precise dependencies given that all the values needed to generate a specialized identifier are known at the time of closure creation.

The mechanism for equality and for caching with precise dependencies now allows us to outline the closure-memoization algorithm. This section first presents the basic closure-memoization algorithm. It then proceeds to describe the complications that arise with continuations and the mechanisms developed to allow closure-memoization to be effective. In essence, continuations cannot be stored in closures for memoization to be effective. This follows from observing that a function's continuation is necessarily different each time it is called and, therefore, any closure that captures that continuation will necessarily be different at each call. In addition, the last-in first-out discipline of continuations provides compiler writers with the choice to heap-allocate and memoize or to not heap-allocate and not memoize continuation-closures.

3.1   Basic Closure Memoization

To illustrate the salient closure memoization features, consider the following function used in the naive solution to the graph isomorphism problem:

```
;map-neighs: (listof nodes) dict -> (listof nodes)
(define map-neighs (lambda (lon d)
                    (map (lambda (i) (name-mapper i d)) lon)))
```

In this solution, for two graphs with n nodes, all $n!$ possible mappings are tested. For each possible mapping, the function map-neighs is called for each of the n nodes. This function takes as input a list of nodes (the neighbors) and a mapping (i.e., a dictionary representing the mapping) and returns a list of (the mapped) nodes.

For a given mapping, m_1, a closure for

```
(lambda (i) (name-mapper i m1))
```

is allocated n times (once for each node). Observe that all n closures are exactly the same for a given m_1: d bound to d_1 (the heap address of m_1) and a pointer to the body of the lambda expression, say L_1. This leads to a total allocation of $n * n!$ closures to test all possible mappings.

For the first call to map-neighs with m_1, using closure memoization, a closure is allocated and cached as, say, $d_1 - L_1$. This closure is then re-used for all subsequent calls to map-neighs with m_1. Under this strategy, the number of closures allocated is reduced to $n!$ from $n * n!$. Even for modest values of n the savings in the number of closure allocations is significant.

3.2 Closure Memoization in the Presence of Continuations

The general outline for basic closure memoization of the previous subsection is not the complete story. The compiler must do a bit more work to memoize closures in the presence of continuations. In particular, it must treat user-defined and continuation function construction and application differently. This is best illustrated using an example. Consider the function map-neighs (λ-lifted and) transformed to continuation-passing style:

```
(define map-neighs
  (lambda (a0 a1 V)
    (F0 name-mapper
        a1
        (lambda (V0) (map V0 a0 V)))))

(define F0
  (lambda (name-mapper a1 V)
    (V (lambda (a2 V0) (name-mapper a2 a1 V0)))))
```

Intuitively, as before, we expect $n!$ closures to be allocated when memoization is used. Our intuitive expectations are not met, because one of the free variables, V, stored in the created closures is a continuation. Recall, that a continuation is, in essence, a function to compute the value of the rest of the computation. Therefore, each call to map-neighs with a mapping, m_1, is made with a different continuation and allocates a different closure. None of the closures are re-used and we have a total of $n * n!$ closures allocated under closure memoization.

This situation is precisely where memoization becomes ineffective. Memoization is predicated on repetition. Intuitively, we can see that there is repetition in the calls to map-neighs with m_1. That is, a lot of the same information is stored in the different closures. Specifically, the binding of m_1 and the pointer to the body of the λ-expression. These values would be captured and shared, instead of copied, by safely-linked closures.

The key to success, therefore, is to isolate these repetitive components from the non-repetitive components (akin to what is done by safely-linked closures). That is, continuations cannot be stored in closures. Thus, providing the opportunity to memoize the repetitive nature that exists in continuation-closure construction. For noncontinuation-closures, this is not an issue given that these closures never store a continuation. They only receive a continuation as input as the reader can observe in the nested λ in F0.

Fortunately, CPS allows us to not store continuations in continuation-closures. CPS serializes computations by making control explicit. Continuations, simply stated, are accumulators for control information. As such, the last continuation constructed is always the first continuation applied [14]. There is nothing in this control mechanism that forces us to explicitly pass control information to every user-defined function. Instead, control information (i.e., the continuation) can be an implicit argument much like the heap is an implicit argument.

To achieve this, the compiler must generate code to construct continuation-closures that differs from code generated to construct noncontinuation-closures. When a continuation-closure is constructed, the enclosing continuation is not stored in it. Instead, it is stored in an accumulator for continuations. In Green, we have two possible flat-closure representations for continuation-closures. In the first, references to heap-allocated continuation-closures are stored in the accumulator allowing for memoization. In the second, continuation-closures are represented as a collection of heap references (to the bindings of free variables) that are directly stored in the accumulator (without allocating a closure data structure in the heap). This implementation strategy reduces the amount of heap memory that must be explicitly garbage collected at the expense of disallowing continuation-closure memoization (if it is not permanently allocated in the heap, then it can not be memoized). One clear consequence of this second representation choice is that it eliminates the overhead of closure memoization for continuations. Regardless of the representation, if c_i and c_j are the last and next to last continuations accumulated, then the enclosing continuation for c_i is c_j. If a new continuation, c_h, is constructed then it is added to this accumulator in front of c_i. When a continuation is applied, the top continuation, say c_h, is removed and applied to its argument. Its enclosing continuation, c_i, then becomes the top continuation in the accumulator.

At runtime a hash table is used to store references to heap-allocated closures. Instead of allocating a closure and then populating it when a closure is constructed, the values needed to create the closure are accumulated. As the values are accumulated, the unique descriptor is constructed. When a closure constructor is executed, descriptor membership in the hash table is tested (i.e., equality is tested). If the closure exists, a new closure is not allocated, the accumulated values are discarded, and the previously generated closure is used. If the closure does not exist, a new closure is allocated in the heap using the accumulated values and the new closure is added to the hash table. This mechanism is the same for both continuation- and noncontinuation-closures when both are heap-allocated. If continuation-closures are not heap-allocated, then their construction dispenses with the creation of the unique identifier and the use of the hash table. The creation of the unique key and the testing of hash table membership adds overhead to the flat closure creation mechanism. To achieve speed-ups, this overhead must be effectively amortized over the number of times closures are re-used.

4   The Green Programming Language and Virtual Machine

Before examining empirical data, the Green programming language and the GVM are briefly described. Green is a functional, eager, and impure programming

$$program ::= (def^*)$$
$$def ::= (\textbf{define } symbol \ expr)$$
$$expr ::= symbol \mid number \mid boolean \mid string$$
$$\mid \ (\textbf{list } expr^*) \mid (\textbf{array } expr^*) \mid (\textbf{quote } symbol)$$
$$\mid \ (\lambda \ (symbol^*) \ expr) \mid (\lambda_c \ (symbol^*) \ expr)$$
$$\mid \ (\textbf{let } ((symbol \ expr)^*) \ expr) \mid (\textbf{if } expr \ expr \ expr)$$
$$\mid \ (\textbf{set! } expr \ expr) \mid (\textbf{begin } expr^*)$$
$$\mid \ (primitive \ expr^*) \mid (expr^+) \mid (\textbf{apply-cont } expr \ expr)$$

Fig. 1. The Green core language

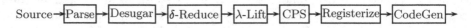

Fig. 2. The architecture of the CPS-based Green compiler.

language. Although mutation is supported, its use is, in general, discouraged favoring mutation-free programming whenever possible. The syntax of the Green core language is displayed in Fig. 1[2]. A program is a list of definitions. A definition binds a symbol to the value of an expression. An expression can either be a variable, a primitive value (e.g., number, boolean, string, or symbol), a list, an array, a function definition (i.e., a λ-expression), an expression with local declarations (i.e., a let-expression), a conditional, an assignment statement, a sequencing statement (i.e., a begin-expression), or a primitive/function application. In addition, since continuations are treated differently from user-defined functions, an expression can be a continuation definition (i.e., a λ_c-expression) or a continuation application (i.e., an apply-cont-expression). Through the process of desugaring [20], a much richer source syntax is presented to programmers. This source language allows users to have, for example, nested definitions, general conditionals (i.e., cond-expressions), and/or-expressions, quoted lists, structure definitions, and quasiquoted lists.

The Green compiler (implemented in Racket) transforms a program written in source syntax into bytecode for the GVM. The architecture of the compiler is displayed in Fig. 2. Source syntax is parsed and desugared. The desugaring process eliminates all non-core expressions. In addition, all let expressions are transformed into function applications. The let-free program is then δ-reduced transforming expressions to normal form whenever possible. After δ-reduction, the program is transformed using λ-lifting [21,22]. After this step, all functions are defined at the top level. If a function does not contain free variables the definition contains a λ-expression with a body that is not a λ-expression. If the function has free variables, then there is a nested λ-expression. The outer λ-expression has the free variables as parameters. The nested λ has as parameters those specified in the source program. A λ-expression does not appear elsewhere in the program. This means that we precisely know when a user-defined func-

---

[2] The use of bold type signals a reserved word.

tion is being compiled (as opposed to a continuation) and what free variables are needed to construct a closure. After λ-lifting, the program is transformed to continuation-passing style. This step adds a continuation parameter to all functions and adds a continuation argument to all application expressions. The continuation argument is always a variable-expression or a λ_c-expression which, technically speaking, undoes the work of λ-lifting. For our purposes, however, this is precisely the goal. A λ_c-expression indicates that a continuation, not a user-defined function, is being compiled. In addition, wherever the source program returns an expressed value it now returns the result of applying the continuation to that expressed value. The expressed value can be a closure which means that a λ-expression can be an argument to a λ_c-expression. The CPS program is then registerized eliminating function parameters in favor of using registers to pass values to functions. To further aid the compilation process, let-expressions are reintroduced. The body of a let expression must be a λ_c-expression and the local variable declarations capture the free variables of the continuation. Thus, we precisely know how to build the closure for the continuation with or without closure memoization. In addition, function calls are implemented as GOTOs given that they all appear in tail position. Finally, the code generator transforms the registerized program to bytecode for the GVM. A flag indicates to the code generator whether or not closure memoization is desired.

The GVM is, in essence, a bytecode interpreter (written in C++) that manages a heap from which memory is dynamically allocated at runtime. It has a set of registers that are used for parameter passing. These registers must be set correctly to transfer control to a function being called as the GVM has no mechanism for returning from a function call. That is, the GVM assumes that there are no delayed operations in the code produced by the compiler as is expected for programs written in CPS. Heap elements all consist of five bytes: a one-byte tag and a four-byte value. Values are either literals or a reference to other heap-allocated values. A closure requires a header that has a closure tag and a reference to the compiled body of a λ-expression or λ_c-expression. This 5-byte header is followed in the heap by an array of references to the free variable bindings (each a 5-byte heap element). There is no need to store a reference to this array in the heap element representing a closure.

A novel feature of the GVM is that it maintains a hash table for the management of memoized closures. If closures are not memoized, the hash table is not used. To memoize a closure, as previously stated, a descriptor (i.e., a unique key to be hashed) is created. If the descriptor exists in the closure hash table, then the closure is not created and the previously generated closure is used. If the key does not exist in the closure hash table, then the closure is allocated and added to the hash table. The construction of a descriptor adds overhead to memoized-closure allocation. This overhead, however, is amortized over less closure creation. If memory allocation is significantly less, then this overhead on closure construction is justified even in the absence of garbage collection.

When continuations are not memoized, references to the values of the free variables are stored in a heap-allocated stack. The stack itself is allocated in

```
f
    ALLOC 2 L_gencodeFL0      ;;;Allocates continuation of size 2
    FVC 0 R1                  ;;;Copy free variable 0 from R1
    FVC 1 R2                  ;;;Copy free variable 1 from R2
    POP R1                    ;;;pop continuation into R1
    GOTO g                    ;;;go to code for g
L_gencodeFL0
    FVACC 0                   ;;;access free variable 0 in current closure
    PUSHREG R0                ;;;push register 0 onto stack
    *                         ;;;multiply together
    POP R0                    ;;;pop answer into R0
    FVACC 1                   ;;;access free varaible 1 (continuation)
    GOTOFV                    ;;;goto continuation
```

Fig. 3. Bytecode when closures are not memoized and continuations are explicit.

contiguous heap addresses to allow automatic recycling of memory for continuations without the interference of a garbage collector. This implementation choice is justifiable if the amount of heap memory not automatically recycled (without the interference of a garbage collector) is significantly reduced and/or speed-ups are observed.

To make the compilation more concrete consider compiling the following function already transformed to CPS:

```
(define (f x y k)
  (g x (lambda (a) (k (* y a)))))
```

Figure 3 displays the generated bytecode when closures are not memoized and continuations are explicit. The bytecode for f allocates a closure of size 2 to store the free variables, y and k, for the nested lambda (i.e., the continuation). The bindings of these free variables are, respectively, stored in registers 1 and 2 when f is called and are, respectively, copied into the closure at positions 0 and 1. A reference to the closure is placed into register 1 as it is the second argument to g. There is no need to do anything for the first argument to g, x, as it is already in register 0 (given that it is the first parameter to f). Finally, the bytecode transfers control to g. The bytecode for the nested lambda accesses the value of y in position 0 of the closure and the argument to the continuation in register 0, multiplies them, and places the product in register 0 in preparation for the call to k. The saved continuation, k, is retrieved from the closure, where it is stored in position 1, and control is transferred to it.

Figure 4 displays the bytecode generated when all closures are memoized. The byetcode for f starts building the name of the closure by accessing y in register 1. As it is the only free variable (recall that continuations are not stored in closures), the continuation constructor (i.e., CONT) checks if the continuation already exists. If so, it returns it. If not, it allocates it using the binding for y. Finally, the bytecode transfers control to g. The bytecode for the nested lambda multiplies y, stored in position 0 of the closure, and (g x), the only parameter to

```
f
    FVC2 0 R1                ;;;begin building closure name with R1
    CONT 1 L_gencodeFL0      ;;;continuation constructor
    GOTO g                   ;;;go to g
L_gencodeFL0
    FVACC 0                  ;;;access free variable 0
    PUSHREG R0               ;;;push register 0 onto stack
    *                        ;;;multiply
    POP R0                   ;;;pop answer into R0
    GOTOCS                   ;;;invoke the top continuation
```

Fig. 4. Bytecode when all closures are memoized.

```
f
    SCONT 1 L_gencodeFL0     ;;;allocates continuation on stack
    CFVC 0 R1                ;;;copies R1 to closure at position 0
    GOTO g                   ;;;transfers control to g
L_gencodeFL0
    FVACC 0                  ;;;access free variable 0
    PUSHREG R0               ;;;push R0 onto the stack
    *                        ;;;multiply
    POP R0                   ;;;pop into R0
    GOTOCS                   ;;;transfers control to top continuation
```

Fig. 5. Bytecode when only non-continuation closures are memoized.

the continuation which is stored in register 0, placing the product in register 0 in preparation for the invocation of the continuation. Finally, control is transferred to the top continuation on the continuation stack.

Figure 5 displays the bytecode generated when only non-continuation closures are memoized. The bytecode for f allocates a closure of size one directly on the continuation stack. The binding of the free variable, y, is copied to the closure and control is transferred to g. The bytecode for the nested lambda accesses, as before, y and a, multiplies them, and places the product in register 0. Control is then transferred to the top continuation and its closure is popped of the stack. No memory footprint remains of the popped continuation as the memory it occupies is immediately recycled and made available for future use in the continuation stack.

5   Empirical Measurements

This section presents empirical measurements taken using three non-trivial benchmarks. The benchmarks include:

MM This benchmark multiplies two 50×50 matrices of random fixed-sized integers. The matrix is represented as a list of columns. The well-known formula, $r_{ij} = a_i \cdot b^j$, is used to compute the result. That is, the entry of the ith row and j^{th} column of the result is the dot product of the ith row of A and the jth column of B [23].

TSP This benchmark solves the NP-complete Traveling Salesman Problem [24]. The input is, K_6, the complete graph of 6 nodes. The graph is represented as an adjacency list of nodes with weighted edges. The first node in the graph is considered the start/end node. The algorithm generates all permutations of possible intermediate nodes and returns the valid path, if any, with the smallest weight.

GI This benchmark determines if two graphs are isomorphic. This problem is not known to be NP-complete and it is not known to have a polynomial-time solution [25]. The inputs given are two complete graphs, K_7, with 7 nodes. The algorithm checks to see if both graphs have the same number of nodes. If so, all mappings of nodes in the second graph to the nodes in the first graph are checked to see if any generate the same lists of corresponding edges in the second graph.

The data collected analyzes the impact of closure memoization along four fronts: total number of closures allocated, running time, total number of noncontinuation closures allocated, and heap size after execution. Each benchmark was executed using the three implementation strategies described: Non-Memoized (i.e., traditional flat closures implement λ and λ_c expressions), All Closures Memoized (i.e., all λ and λ_c expressions are implemented using heap-allocated closures that are memoized), and Noncontinuation Closures Memoized (i.e., λ expressions are implemented as memoized heap-allocated closures and λ_c expressions are implemented as a collection of references on the stack). Finally, all benchmarks were executed to termination without the interference of a garbage collector.

Figure 6 displays the total number of heap-allocated closures for each implementation strategy. This data is presented using a log-based scale (i.e., the y-axis). The strategy that does not memoize closures always allocates the most closures: about 10^6 for all benchmarks. The second best strategy is the one that memoizes all closures. For this strategy, when compared with traditional flat closures, we observe about one order of magnitude fewer heap-allocated closures for MM, about two orders of magnitude fewer heap-allocated closures for TSP, and less than an order of magnitude fewer heap-allocated closures for GI. To no surprise, the strategy that exhibits the fewest heap-allocated closures is the one that only heap-allocates and memoizes noncontinuation-closures (i.e., λ-expressions). The data clearly establishes that the bulk of the closures that are heap-allocated are for continuations, as expected for a CPS representation, and that not heap-allocating (and not memoizing) continuations significantly reduces the memory footprint of closures.

Figure 7 displays the relative difference in running time between using traditional flat closures and the other two implementation strategies. The x-axis represents the running time using traditional flat closures. A positive relative difference indicates that the use of traditional flat closures is slower and is represented by a bar above the x-axis. A negative relative difference indicates that the use of traditional flat closures is faster and is represented by a bar below

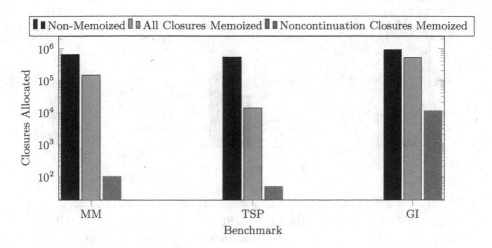

Fig. 6. Total number of heap-allocated closures.

the x-axis. Memoizing all closures produces better running times for MM (about 1%) and for TSP (about 8%). For GI, we observe that memoizing all closures increases execution time (by about 7%). The observed performance is explained by the effectiveness of memoization. In Fig. 6, we observed that memoizing all closures is much more effective for MM and TSP. This means that the overhead incurred by memoization is well-amortized over the gains obtained from fewer closures being allocated. In contrast, the relatively modest gains in the reduction in closure allocation for GI do not suffice to overcome this overhead and cause this benchmark to run slower.

Figure 7 also shows that all benchmarks run faster than using traditional flat closures when only heap-allocating and memoizing noncontinuation closures. MM is about 5% faster, TSP is about 15% faster, and GI is about 10% faster. These are significant gains in execution time. We can also observe that only heap-allocating and memoizing noncontinuation-closures is also faster for all benchmarks when compared to heap-allocating and memoizing all closures. The explanation for this observed performance is at least three-fold. First, we observe that noncontinuation-closures are effectively memoized (i.e., there is significant reuse of noncontinuation-closures) while continuation-closures are not effectively memoized. Second, pushing and popping continuations closures from the stack is faster that heap allocation. Third, the frequent access to the top of the continuation stack is likely to exhibit better cache behavior than heap allocated data.

Figure 7 also reveals that that all benchmarks run faster only heap-allocating and memoizing noncontinuation closures when compared to memoizing all closures. It is about 4% faster for MM, about 8% faster for TSP, and about 18% faster for GI. The observed speed-ups are remarkably good. The explanation for this is that memoized continuations are not re-used enough to justify memoizing them. This means that the overhead of memoizing continuations has a substantial impact on execution time. Put differently, the memoization overhead for

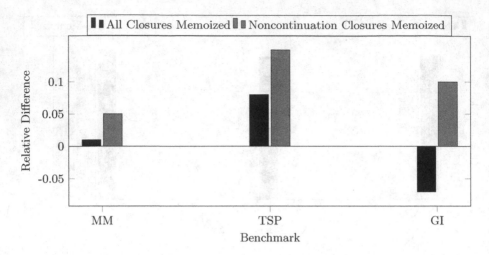

Fig. 7. Running time relative difference.

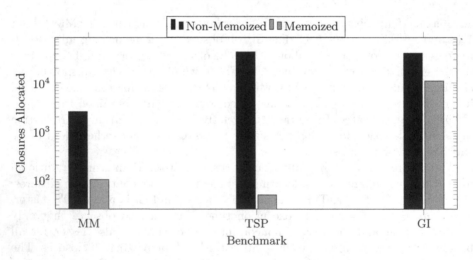

Fig. 8. Total number of noncontinuation closures allocated.

continuations is not effectively amortized over the number of times continuations are re-used.

Figure 8 displays the total number of noncontinuation-closures allocated when they are not memoized and when they are memoized. The data is presented using a log-based scale. For all benchmarks, we see a significant reduction in non-continuation closures allocated: one order of magnitude for MM, three orders of magnitude for TSP, and almost an order of magnitude for GI. These differences explain why memoization overhead is effectively amortized over closure reuse leading to, in part, the speed-ups observed in Fig. 7. This data suggests that closure memoization ought to be an effective strategy for non-CPS-based compilers that generate code that only allocates noncontinuation closures. This hypothesis,

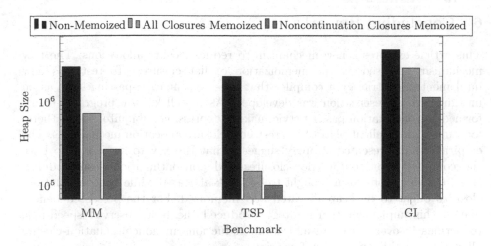

Fig. 9. Heap size after execution.

of course, needs to be validated with empirical studies that, for instance, use an ANF-based compiler.

Figure 9 displays the memory footprint (i.e., total number of allocated heap elements after execution) for each benchmark using all three closure implementation strategies. Not surprisingly, traditional flat closures have the largest footprint. Memoizing all closures has the next best memory footprint. When compared to traditional flat closures, memoizing all closures exhibits a reduction of one order of magnitude for MM, one order of magnitude for TSP, and less than one order of magnitude for GI. The best footprint observed is from only heap-allocating and memoizing noncontinuation closures. When compared to traditional flat closures, we see one order of magnitude reduction for MM, two orders of magnitude for TSP, and less than one order of magnitude for GI. This data brings us back to garbage collection. Allocating continuation-closures on a stack to automatically recycle their memory with every pop operation and memoizing noncontinuation closures is the most effective strategy to reduce the memory footprint of the observed programs. This means that the amount of work and the number of times a garbage collector must be invoked is reduced.

In conclusion, the data presented strongly suggests that the best closure implementation strategy based on flat closures is to only memoize noncontinuation closures and to stack-allocate continuation closures. The data empirically validates the strategy pioneered by the Orbit compiler to stack-allocate continuation-closures. It also suggests that flat closure memoization is a viable and important optimization for CPS-based compilers and may also be an important optimization for non-CPS based compilers. It is noteworthy, that the data bears out the historical trend that continuation-closures must be treated differently from noncontinuation-closures and that flat closure memoization is yet another step towards making functional languages interact even better with garbage collectors.

6   Concluding Remarks

This article explores a new mechanism to reduce closure allocations. The new mechanism is based on the memoization of flat closures. To test this new implementation strategy a compiler that uses continuation-passing style as an intermediate representation was developed. As is well known, programs transformed to continuation-passing style make λ-expressions ubiquitous and, therefore, make an excellent platform to test new closure allocation mechanisms. The empirical data presented strongly suggests that the key to success is to have the compiler treat continuation-closures and noncontinuation-closures differently. Continuation-closures ought to be stack-allocated while noncontinuation-closures ought to be heap-allocated and memoized. For the presented benchmarks, this implementation strategy produced the best observed speed-ups, reductions in overall closure allocation, reductions in noncontinuation-closure allocations, and heap memory footprint.

There are several natural lines for long term future work. The first is to continue the process of memoization by memoizing applications of closures to arguments. If successful, in addition to the benefits of flat closure memoization, programs will perform less computation. Another important and new line of research that rises from this work is the development of a garbage collector for memoized closures. There is a large spectrum of possibilities to explore that ranges from always considering memoized closures not in the live set to using heuristics to decide which memoized closures to consider garbage to only garbage collecting memoized closures if necessary. Future work also includes measuring the impact of memoized flat closures for an ANF-based compiler. Finally, part of our future work will study the elimination of flat closures in favor of generating memoized bytecode at runtime using a controlled form of β-reduction [26].

Acknowledgements. The Physics Nobel Laureate, Richard Feynman, was once asked to explain why spin one-half particles obey Fermi Dirac statistics [27]. He rose to the challenge and responded that he will prepare a freshman lecture on it. A few days later he returned and stated that "I could not do it. I could not reduce it to the freshman level. That means we really don't understand it." The authors thank the Computer Science Department at Seton Hall University for their support that made the development of this work possible and for their support of our continuing efforts to make this material understandable to young and upcoming computer scientists.

References

1. Patterson, D.A., Hennessy, J.L.: Computer Organization and Design: The Hardware/Software Interface, 5th edn. Morgan Kaufmann Publishers Inc., San Francisco (2013)
2. Wilson, P.R.: Uniprocessor garbage collection techniques. In: Bekkers, Y., Cohen, J. (eds.) IWMM 1992. LNCS, vol. 637, pp. 1–42. Springer, Heidelberg (1992). https://doi.org/10.1007/BFb0017182

3. Serrano, M., Boehm, H.J.: Understanding memory allocation of scheme programs. In: Odersky, M., Wadler, P. (eds.) Proceedings of the Fifth International Conference on Functional Programming, pp. 245–256. ACM (2000)
4. Zorn, B.: The measured cost of conservative garbage collection. Softw. Pract. Exp. **23**(7), 733–756 (1993)
5. Henderson, P.: Functional Programming: Application and Implementation. Prentice-Hall International, Englewood (1980)
6. Landin, P.J.: The mechanical evaluation of expressions. Comput. J. **6**(4), 308–320 (1964)
7. Kent Dybvig, R.: The development of Chez Scheme. In: Proceedings of the Eleventh ACM SIGPLAN International Conference on Functional Programming, pp. 1–12, September 2006
8. Cardelli, L.: Compiling a functional language. In: Proceedings of the 1984 ACM Conference on LISP and Functional Programming, pp. 208–217 (1984)
9. Shao, Z., Appel, A.W.: Space-efficient closure representations. Technical report CS-TR-454-94, Department of Computer Science, Princeton University, Princeton (1994)
10. Shivers, O.: Control-flow analysis of higher-order languages of taming lambda. Ph.D. thesis, School of Computer Science, Carnegie Mellon University, Pittsburgh, May 1991
11. Steele Jr., G.L.: Rabbit: a compiler for scheme. Technical report, Massachusetts Institute of Technology, Cambridge (1978)
12. Adams, N., Kranz, D., Kelsey, R., Rees, J., Hudak, P., Philbin, J.: ORBIT: an optimizing compiler for scheme. In: Proceedings of the 1986 SIGPLAN Symposium on Compiler Construction, SIGPLAN 1986, pp. 219–233. ACM, New York (1986)
13. Kelsey, R., Hudak, P.: Realistic compilation by program transformation (detailed summary). In: Proceedings of the 16th ACM SIGPLAN-SIGACT Symposium on Principles of Programming Languages, POPL 1989, pp. 281–292. ACM, New York (1989)
14. Appel, A.W.: Compiling with Continuations. Cambridge University Press, New York (2007)
15. Flanagan, C., Sabry, A., Duba, B.F., Felleisen, M.: The essence of compiling with continuations. In: Proceedings of the ACM SIGPLAN 1993 Conference on Programming Language Design and Implementation, PLDI 1993, pp. 237–247. ACM, New York (1993)
16. Flanagan, C., Sabry, A., Duba, B.F., Felleisen, M.: The essence of compiling with continuations. SIGPLAN Not. **39**(4), 502–514 (2004)
17. Kennedy, A.: Compiling with continuations, continued. In: Proceedings of the 12th ACM SIGPLAN International Conference on Functional Programming, ICFP 2007, pp. 177–190. ACM, New York (2007)
18. Fluet, M., Weeks, S.: Contification using dominators. In: Proceedings of the Sixth ACM SIGPLAN International Conference on Functional Programming, ICFP 2001, pp. 2–13. ACM, New York (2001)
19. Acar, U.A., Blelloch, G.E., Harper, R.: Selective memoization. In: Proceedings of the 30th Annual ACM Symposium on Principles of Programming Languages, pp. 14–25. ACM Press (2003)
20. Krishnamurthi, S.: Desugaring in practice: opportunities and challenges. In: Proceedings of the 2015 Workshop on Partial Evaluation and Program Manipulation, PEPM 2015, pp. 1–2. ACM, New York (2015)

21. Johnsson, T.: Lambda lifting: transforming programs to recursive equations. In: Jouannaud, J.-P. (ed.) FPCA 1985. LNCS, vol. 201, pp. 190–203. Springer, Heidelberg (1985). https://doi.org/10.1007/3-540-15975-4_37
22. Morazán, M.T., Schultz, U.P.: Optimal lambda lifting in quadratic time. In: Chitil, O., Horváth, Z., Zsók, V. (eds.) IFL 2007. LNCS, vol. 5083, pp. 37–56. Springer, Heidelberg (2008). https://doi.org/10.1007/978-3-540-85373-2_3
23. Venit, S., Bishop, W.: Elementary Linear Algebra, 2nd edn. Prindle, Weber & Schmidt, Boston (1985)
24. Lewis, H.R., Papadimitriou, C.H.: Elements of the Theory of Computation, 2nd edn. Prentice Hall PTR, Upper Saddle River (1997)
25. Köbler, J., Schöning, U., Torán, J.: The Graph Isomorphism Problem: Its Structural Complexity. Birkhauser Verlag, Basel (1993)
26. Morazán, M.T.: Bytecode and memoized closure performance. In: McCarthy, J. (ed.) TFP 2013. LNCS, vol. 8322, pp. 58–75. Springer, Heidelberg (2014). https://doi.org/10.1007/978-3-642-45340-3_4
27. Goldstein, D.L.: Richard P. Feynman, teacher. Phys. Today **42**(2), 70–75 (1989)

Maintaining Separation of Concerns Through Task Oriented Software Development

Jurriën Stutterheim, Peter Achten[⊠], and Rinus Plasmeijer

Institute for Computing and Information Sciences,
Radboud University Nijmegen, Nijmegen, The Netherlands
{j.stutterheim,p.achten,rinus}@cs.ru.nl

Abstract. Task Oriented Programming is a programming paradigm that enhances 'classic' functional programming with means to express the coordination of work among people and computer systems, the distribution and control of data sources, and the human-machine interfaces. To make the creation process of such applications feasible, it is important to have separation of concerns. In this paper we demonstrate how this is achieved within the Task Oriented Software Development process and illustrate the approach by means of a case study.

1 Introduction

In software development, it is well known that achieving *separation of concerns* is instrumental in creating well structured software. The reason is that by *"focussing one's attention upon some aspect"* [10] software developers put themselves in a better position to ascertain that they are constructing the intended software in the correct way. A guideline to obtain this is to *"design your software so that each unit or component does one thing and one thing only"* [25]. Figure 1a illustrates a common text book approach that uses layers to structure applications. The *resource access layer* is concerned with all external, temporary, and persistent information sources; the concern of the *business layer* is the application workflow; the *presentation layer*'s concern is the design and implementation of the UI. When applied in a strict way, each layer relies only on the interface offered by the one immediately below it. For efficiency this is sometimes relaxed.

Task Oriented Programming (TOP) [19,23] is a functional style programming paradigm with a software development approach (Task Oriented Software Development) that deals with separation of concerns in a novel way. This is illustrated in Fig. 1b. For each of the above mentioned concerns, it introduces one core *type-parameterized concept*: *shared data sources* (SDS) for the remote access layer, *tasks* for the business layer, and *UI* modeling for the presentation layer. Instead of hiding the application entities and their relations – the *Universe of Discourse* (UoD) – within the business layer, in TOP the UoD is modeled explicitly and separately. This is done by identifying the entities via

© Springer International Publishing AG, part of Springer Nature 2018
M. Wang and S. Owens (Eds.): TFP 2017, LNCS 10788, pp. 19–38, 2018.
https://doi.org/10.1007/978-3-319-89719-6_2

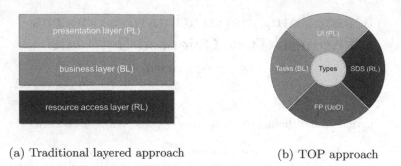

(a) Traditional layered approach   (b) TOP approach

Fig. 1. Separation of concerns

data structures and the relations that exist between entities via pure functions. Hence, this can be done by traditional functional programming. As a result, TOP enhances functional programming with type-parameterized concepts that handle their concerns in a better way than a singular functional programming solution can. TOP is not a layered approach. Instead, UoD elements, SDS's, tasks, and UI modeling can use each other where appropriate, which motivates our choice to illustrate this by means of a pie-chart shape. In TOP types have a pivotal function. Types convey sufficient information for a TOP implementation to generate all boilerplate code that comes with programming applications: (G)UI generation, data (de)serialization, and code distribution. As a result, a TOP program(mer) is not concerned with these issues. Instead, the above mentioned concepts suffice to generate a complete application. For this reason, TOP is an example of type-driven model based software development.

Task Oriented Software Development (TOSD) is the TOP software development approach (Sect. 2). It has emerged from a number of case studies. Some of them have been reported in [19] and concern case studies performed in collaboration with the Dutch coast guard [18,20]. In other case studies we have investigated the development of distributed games [2,3].

In this paper we show how TOSD achieves separation of concerns (Sect. 3). We present a small, yet realistic, case study that we have conducted for the Dutch tax authorities. The case study is implemented in the iTasks framework [24] that implements TOP as a Domain Specific Language (DSL), shallowly embedded in the host language Clean to create distributed, multi-user, web-applications. It uses *generic programming* [5,15] and *dynamic types* [26] to satisfy the type driven requirement of the TOP paradigm. iTasks is not the only TOP implementation: μTasks [21] is a Haskell embedded TOP DSL implementation for interruptible embedded systems, and mTasks, currently under development, is a Clean based TOP implementation for IoT devices [16]. In the remainder of the paper we discuss related work (Sect. 4), and conclude (Sect. 5).

2   Task Oriented Software Development

TOSD distinguishes the following phases that are related one-to-one with the TOP concepts illustrated in Fig. 1b: (1) *UoD Modeling*, (2) *SDS Modeling*, (3) *Task Modeling*, and (4) *UI Modeling*. TOSD does not impose or assume a particular software engineering discipline, such as waterfall, agile, or evolutionary software development [25]. It can be used in any of these approaches. The TOSD phases can be implemented in any order. In our experience it is advisable to start with the UoD Modeling phase because the entity types and relations serve as input for the type-driven model based software development approach of TOP and TOSD. Next, SDS Modeling and Task Modeling are iteratively applied to identify the (local) data sources and the (computational and user-) tasks that need to be accomplished in the application. Often, this also involves the UoD to get improved along the way. It is important to note that at any point in time, during these phases, one has access to a working application that is generated by the TOP implementation. In particular, all UI elements are generated and task distribution is taken care of. This makes the approach particularly useful for exploration, rapid prototyping, and iterative software development. Finally, UI Modeling is applied to obtain the proper UI 'screens' and layout.

The rest of this section describes the individual TOSD phases in more detail. Each phase starts with a phrase that describes its key concern.

2.1   UoD Modeling

Concerns the acquisition of the 'vocabulary' of the application domain. The purpose of this phase is establish a common ground between the stakeholders of the application and the developers. The vocabulary is obtained via stakeholder interviews and investigation of the application domain. *Entities* are modeled using the host language *data types*, while the *entity-relations* are modeled using *pure functions*. Developing a TOP program starts off the same way as any functional program. However, for defining side-effects, I/O, user interfaces, communication, synchronization, TOP concepts are used instead of familiar FP techniques.

The absence of side-effects in the resulting domain model ensures that this part of the code can be tested and maintained using best-practices such as Test-Driven Development and Type-Driven Development.

2.2   SDS Modeling

Concerns the identification of existing or needed sources of information. The purpose of this phase is to identify the sources of information without committing oneself to how, when, or by what and whom these are used. Sharing information typically increases the opportunities for collaboration.

Shared Data Sources [12] (Fig. 2) are type-parameterized interfaces to information sources. With a SDS of type RWShared p r w, information is read as a value of type r, and written as a value of type w. The *focus domain* p controls the amount of information that is transferred, which is vital in case of large

```
:: RWShared p r w  // is an opaque type
:: SDS          r w :== RWShared () r w
:: Shared       a  :== SDS a a
// SDS combinators:
(>*<)     :: (RWShared p a b)  (RWShared p c d) -> RWShared p (a,c) (b,d) | iTask p
mapRead  :: (    r -> r')      (RWShared p r w) -> RWShared p r' w        | iTask p
mapWrite :: (w' r -> Maybe w) (RWShared p r w) -> RWShared p r  w'        | iTask p
// SDS access:
get       ::              (SDS r w) -> Task r | iTask r
set       ::        w (SDS r w) -> Task w | iTask w
upd       :: (r -> w) (SDS r w) -> Task w | iTask r & iTask w
watch     ::              (SDS r w) -> Task r | iTask r
// predefined SDS:
currentDate :: SDS Date ()
```

Fig. 2. Fragment of the iTask API concerning SDS Modeling

volumes of data. In this paper this is not used, and instead the simpler versions, SDS and Shared are used. SDSs use a publish-subscribe approach: whenever shared information is changed by someone, those parties who need to be informed are automatically updated. SDSs can be defined globally and locally, thus limiting and protecting their access. Examples of global SDSs are the current time, the current value of sensors on some other system, information stored in data bases, and files on file systems. SDSs are compositional in two directions: some SDS combinators aggregate SDSs, while others allow for projections of information. Examples in Fig. 2 are >*< that combines two SDSs into a paired version, mapRead that alters the read-interface, and mapWrite that alters the write-interface.

2.3 Task Modeling

Concerns the identification of the user and application tasks. The purpose of this phase is to identify who is working on what, the users, task dependencies, required information, and the *interaction points*: what information needs to be exchanged between application and users.

More precisely, a task is a type-parameterized interface expressed as a function that results in a value of opaque type Task a (Fig. 3a). Task functions can have arguments like any other function, and may be higher order: they can have functions and tasks as argument or result. Tasks are opaque and observable at the same time: the type parameter a is used by the opaque task to inform whoever is interested about the current 'progress' of the task by means of a task value of type TaskValue a that can change over time. The type and values are determined by the task. When there is *no value*, the task has no sensible information about its progress. When a task value is *unstable*, the task has sensible information about its progress, but further on, the task value might be different. Finally, when a task value is *stable*, it will no longer change. The monadic style return combinator has a stable task value. The functor operator @ alters the task value but not its stability. Tasks that define interaction points (the task functions with Information in their name) never have a stable task value. Every interaction point comes with a UI that is automatically generated from the type of its task value and that allows the user to *enter*, *view*, or *update* values of the specified type. This value can also reside within a SDS (the task functions that also have Shared in their name) and in that case SDS changes caused by other tasks are also automatically applied to that interaction point.

Tasks are compositional. We first discuss the sequential combinators (Fig. 3b). The core sequential task combinator is *step*, >>*. While a task is running, the OnValue task continuations observe its task value and may automatically trigger the execution of the next task as soon as the first of them computes a Just task. The OnAction task continuation is similar, but requires a user to activate the corresponding Action. A number of standard task continuation function patterns are provided: ifValue only yields a continuation task if the predicate holds for the currently observed task value, ifCond yields a continuation task only if the given condition holds and ignores the currently observed task value, and always ignores everything and simply returns the continuation task. Note that because the latter two patterns ignore the currently observed task value, they typically occur in combination with the OnAction task continuation. The monadic style bind combinators >>= and >>- both make a step when the observed task has a stable task value, but >>= adds an OnAction to allow the user to make this step also when the observed task is unstable. The >>| is the usual derived combinator of >>= that ignores the task value altogether.

The signature of the core parallel task combinator is too extensive to discuss in this paper: it controls a dynamic collection of local and remote tasks that each have access to each other's task values. Instead, we present the derived task combinators that are used in the case study (Fig. 3c). The task value of the -&&- combinator consists of the task values of its sub tasks, if any, and is stable only if both task values are stable. The task value of the -||- combinator is either the first stable task value of its sub tasks, or reflects the most recent unstable task value, if any. The ||- combinator forks the first task, and mirrors only the task value of the second task (vice versa for -||). Finally, the @: combinator forks a remote task and adds it to the work pool of the identified user who can be anyone, have a particular role, or a specific individual. The user decides in what order to work on the tasks in her task pool.

Higher-order tasks encourage developers to create reusable task patterns. In Fig. 4 we show a few of them that are used in the case study. The maybeCancel task adds a 'panic' button to ensure that the user can always force progress. The waitForDate task shows the content of the currentDate SDS (Fig. 2) until a given date. The deadlineWith task adds a parallel task that returns a value after some time, thus ensuring that the combined task always returns a value. The reminder task displays a reminder message after a given date.

```
:: Task a          // is an opaque type
:: TaskValue  a    = NoValue  | Value a Stability
:: Stability       = Unstable | Stable
// Monadic style return:
return             :: a -> Task a | iTask a
// Alter task value and retain stability:
(@) infixl 1       :: (Task a) (a -> b) -> Task b
// Interaction point tasks (see Figure 5 for the Option types):
enterInformation         :: String [EnterOption  m ]              -> Task m | iTask m
viewInformation          :: String [ViewOption    m ]      m     -> Task m | iTask m
updateInformation        :: String [UpdateOption m m]      m     -> Task m | iTask m
viewSharedInformation    :: String [ViewOption    r ] (SDS r w) -> Task r | iTask r
updateSharedInformation  :: String [UpdateOption r w] (SDS r w) -> Task r | iTask r
                                                                    & iTask w
```

(a) Tasks and basic task functions

```
// Step combinator:
(>>*)          :: (Task a) [TaskCont a (Task b)] -> Task b | iTask a & iTask b
:: TaskCont a b = OnValue          ((TaskValue a) -> Maybe b)
                | OnAction Action ((TaskValue a) -> Maybe b) | ...
:: Action      = Action String
// Task continuation functions:
ifValue        :: (a -> Bool) (a -> b) (TaskValue a) -> Maybe b
ifCond         ::         Bool       b  (TaskValue a) -> Maybe b
always         ::                    b  (TaskValue a) -> Maybe b
// Derived combinators of step:
(>>-) infixl 1 :: (Task a) (a -> Task b) -> Task b | iTask a & iTask b
(>>=) infixl 1 :: (Task a) (a -> Task b) -> Task b | iTask a & iTask b
(>>|) infixl 1 :: (Task a)    (Task b) -> Task b | iTask a & iTask b
```

(b) Step combinator and derived combinators

```
// Derived combinators of parallel:
(-&&-) infixr 4   :: (Task a) (Task b) -> Task (a,b) | iTask a & iTask b
(-||-) infixr 3   :: (Task a) (Task a) -> Task  a    | iTask a
(-|| ) infixl 3   :: (Task a) (Task b) -> Task  a    | iTask a & iTask b
( ||-) infixl 3   :: (Task a) (Task b) -> Task  b    | iTask a & iTask b
// Task distribution:
:: UserConstraint = AnyUser | UserWithId UserId | UserWithRole Role
:: UserId        :== String
:: Role          :== String
(@:) :: (UserConstraint,String) (Task a) -> Task a | iTask a
```

(c) Derived parallel combinators

Fig. 3. Fragment of the iTask API concerning Task Modeling

```
maybeCancel :: String (Task a) -> Task (Maybe a) | iTask a
maybeCancel panic t = t >>* [ OnValue  (ifStable            (return o Just) )
                           , OnAction (Action panic) (always (return Nothing)) ]

waitForDate :: Date -> Task Date
waitForDate d
  =    viewSharedInformation ("Wait␣until␣" +++ toString d) [] currentDate
    >>* [OnValue (ifValue (\now -> date < now) return)]

deadlineWith :: Date a (Task a) -> Task a | iTask a
deadlineWith d a t = t -||- (waitForDate d >>| return a)

reminder :: Date String -> Task ()
reminder d m = waitForDate d >>| viewInformation ("Reminder:␣please␣" +++ m) [] ()
```

Fig. 4. Generally useful task patterns

2.4   UI Modeling

Concerns obtaining the appropriate UI experience. The iTasks framework generates for each interaction point a web-based interactive editor task with which the user can construct a proper value of the demanded type for any first order type. The web-based user interfaces work in any HTML5 compatible browser. Because of the type driven approach of TOP, this amounts to deciding the type of information that should be exchanged, knowing that a fully working user interface is generated automatically. This way of working is completely opposite of the more traditional approach of first designing the collection of user interface screens, and develop the program to implement these screens.

```
:: EnterOption  a   = E.v: EnterAs      (v -> a)                        & iTask v
                    | E.v: EnterUsing   (v -> a) (Editor v)             & iTask v
:: ViewOption   a   = E.v: ViewAs       (a -> v)                        & iTask v
                    | E.v: ViewUsing    (a -> v) (Editor v)             & iTask v
:: UpdateOption a b = E.v: UpdateAs     (a -> v) (a v -> b)             & iTask v
                    | E.v: UpdateUsing  (a -> v) (a v -> b) (Editor v) & iTask v
:: SVGEditor m v = { initView :: m -> v, updView :: m v -> v, updModel :: m v -> m
                   , renderImage :: m v *TagSource -> Image v }
fromSVGEditor     :: (SVGEditor v w) -> Editor v | iTask v
```

Fig. 5. Fragment of the iTask API concerning UI Modeling

Automatically generated user interfaces may not always have the right look and feel, so it is necessary that they can be customized. It is important to note that this does not alter the role of the interaction points within the task structures as defined during the Task Modeling phase, but only requires a local change per interaction point that needs to be customized (Fig. 5). In the simplest case, a type is transformed to another type (EnterAs, ViewAs, UpdateAs), after which the generic machinery generates another user interface. A more sophisticated customization can be achieved defining custom client-side *editors* [11] (EnterUsing, ViewUsing, UpdateUsing). One such editor is fromSVGEditor with which a scalable vector graphics (SVG) [9] Image [3] can be created from the required model and view values and keeps them 'in sync' (updView and updModel). Finally, the programmer can overrule the generated layout of task UIs with local annotations [4].

3   Case Study: Solar Panel Tax Compensation

The case has been provided by the Dutch tax authorities and is about a fictional, yet representative, law that enables citizens to apply for tax compensation when they have covered part of their home's roof with solar panels. The execution of this law is done by the Dutch tax authorities. Informally, the solar panel tax compensation law says:

1. the compensation applies only to homes in the Netherlands;
2. the applicant must own the house and reside in it;
3. the solar panels must be of an officially acknowledged type;
4. the solar panels are installed by an officially acknowledged roofing company;
5. the applicant can apply only once every five years per home address.

For rules 1 and 2 the application needs information from *civil affairs* and the *cadastre*. To check rules 3 and 4, the application must have access to a list of acknowledged solar panel types and roofing companies. The latter is maintained by the *chamber of commerce*. Finally, dossiers need to be created and stored to check rule 5. For this particular case, a dossier consists of the applicant's data, invoices and proofs of payment, and a declaration by the roofing company to support the claim. The dossier needs to be completed within three months after the applicant has started the procedure (and a reminder is sent within two months). Completed dossiers are verified by an appropriate tax officer who can either accept or reject, with reason, an application. The applicant is informed, and can, in the latter case, attempt to resubmit the application.

From this specification, we learn that the users are citizens, companies, and tax officers. Besides the tax authorities, information from civil affairs, the chamber of commerce, and the cadastre is required. For each organisation, we introduce a module: Compensation, CivilAffairs, ChamberOfCommerce, Cadastre. We apply TOSD below in the order UoD Modeling (Sect. 3.1), SDS Modeling (Sect. 3.2), Task Modeling (Sect. 3.3), and UI Modeling (Sect. 3.4). In Sect. 3.5, we argue why this case study achieves separation of concerns.

3.1   UoD Modeling

The 'vocabulary' of the application domain is given in Figs. 6 and 7. The relations in these modules are straightforward functions. The *civil affairs* module defines the Citizen entity. Citizens are identified via a social security number

```
definition module CivilAffairs.UoD
import iTasks

:: Citizen
  = { ssn           :: SSN
    , name          :: Name
    , homeAddress :: Maybe Address }
:: NameHomeAddress
  = { name          :: Name
    , homeAddress :: Address }
:: Name
  = { forename      :: String
    , surname       :: String }
:: Address
  = { postcode      :: Postcode
    , houseNumber :: Int }
:: SSN       :== String
:: Postcode :== String
:: Amount    :== Int

citizenFromSSN
    :: SSN [Citizen] -> Maybe Citizen
nameHomeAddressFromCitizen
    :: Citizen -> NameHomeAddress
```

```
definition module ChamberOfCommerce.UoD
import iTasks

:: Company
  = { cocNo    :: COCN
    , cocName :: String
    , type     :: [CompanyType] }
:: COCN        :== String
:: CompanyType :== String

companyHasType
    :: CompanyType Company -> Bool
```

```
definition module Cadastre.UoD

import CivilAffairs.UoD
import ChamberOfCommerce.UoD

:: CadastreRealEstate
  = { address   :: Address
    , mainOwner :: Owner
    , subOwners :: [Owner] }
:: Owner
    :== Either SSN COCN
```

Fig. 6. The UoDs of civil affairs, chamber of commerce, and cadastre

(SSN). The *chamber of commerce* module defines the information regarding companies (Company). They are identified via a chamber of commerce number (COCN). The company type keeps track of the officially registered roles of the company. The *cadastre* module keeps track of all real estate (not only homes). Real estates are identified via their address, and can be owned by citizens and companies.

The chief module Compensation.UoD captures the entities and relations of the solar panel tax compensation. It depends on the entities and relations that are visible through the *cadastre* module. Besides that, it uses the predefined iTasks types Date and Document. A Document is an entity that can be uploaded, which is useful for invoices and photos. The decisionsAfter relation retrieves all relevant decisions concerning a citizen after a given date. The collectionsAfter relation retrieves all collections of a citizen after a given date. The realEstatesOfCitizen relation uses the cadastre information to retrieve all (sub) owned real estate of a citizen and tracks which of these is the home of the citizen. Finally, clientReminderDate and clientDeadlineDate yield the corresponding deadlines of two and three months, using the general purpose relation shiftDate. For the sake of brevity, we do not model entity formats such as social security and chamber of commerce numbers, postcodes, and house numbers. In general, the required level of detail of the UoD is limited only by the stakeholder needs and host language expressiveness.

```
definition module Compensation.UoD
import Cadastre.UoD    // Figure 6

:: RealEstateOwner      = { ownerID            :: Owner
                          , addresses          :: [Address] }
:: OwnedRealEstate      = { isHomeAddress      :: Bool
                          , postcode           :: Postcode
                          , houseNumber        :: Int }
:: Decision             = { ssn                :: SSN
                          , date               :: Date
                          , description        :: String
                          , status             :: DecisionStatus
                          , invoiceAmount       :: Amount
                          , compensation       :: Amount }
:: Collection           = { ssn                :: SSN
                          , description        :: String
                          , date               :: Date
                          , amount             :: Amount }
:: TaxSolarPanelDossier = { request            :: TaxCompensationCitizenRequest
                          , declarationCompany :: CompanyDeclaration
                          , date               :: Date }
:: TaxCompensationCitizenRequest
                        = { ssn                :: SSN
                          , applicant          :: NameHomeAddress
                          , documents          :: TaxCompensationDocuments
                          , company            :: Company }
:: TaxCompensationDocuments
                        = { invoiceAmount      :: Amount
                          , invoiceDate        :: Date
                          , invoiceProof       :: Document
                          , proofOfPayment     :: Document
                          , roofPhotos         :: [Document] }
:: CompanyDeclaration   = { solarPanelType     :: AcceptedSolarPanel
                          , roofPhotos         :: [Document]
                          , roofAreaCovered    :: RoofAreaCovered
                          , date               :: Date }
:: DecisionStatus       = Approved | Rejected Reason
:: Reason               :== String
:: AcceptedSolarPanels  = SolarPanels [AcceptedSolarPanel]
:: AcceptedSolarPanel   :== String
:: RoofAreaCovered      :== Int
:: TimePeriod           = Years Int | Months Int | Days Int

decisionsAfter        :: SSN (DecisionStatus -> Bool) Date [Decision] -> [Decision]
collectionsAfter      :: SSN Date [Collection] -> [Collection]
realEstatesOfCitizen  :: Citizen [CadastreRealEstate] -> [OwnedRealEstate]
shiftDate             :: TimePeriod Date -> Date
clientReminderDate    ::             Date -> Date  // (Months 2)
clientDeadlineDate    ::             Date -> Date  // (Months 3)
```

Fig. 7. The UoD of the solar panel tax compensation

3.2 SDS Modeling

The existing and needed information sources are enumerated in Fig. 8. For simplicity, we assume that civil affairs, chamber of commerce, and cadastre provide access to the citizens, companies, and real estate respectively. The compensation module is split in two groups. The first group of SDSs are storages: keeping track of real estate owned by citizens (realEstateOwners), all decisions (decisions), all collections that need to be payed (collectionPayments) or claimed (collectionClaims), or have been processed (collectionsProcessed), the officially accepted solar panels (acceptedSolarPanels), and finally, all solar panel tax compensation dossiers (solarPanelSubsidyRequests). The second group of SDSs use mapRead (Fig. 2) and an appropriate relation from the compensation UoD (Fig. 7) to obtain information regarding a particular citizen. Here is an example:

currentRealEstate c = mapRead (realEstatesOfCitizen c) cadastreRealEstate

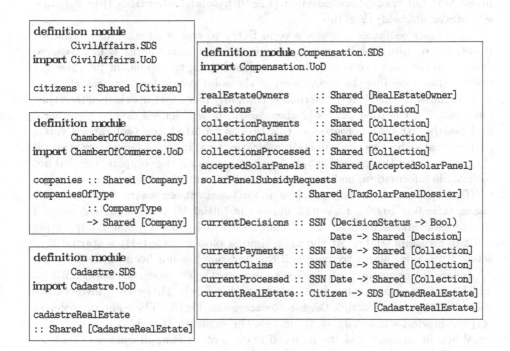

Fig. 8. The SDSs of all organisations

3.3 Task Modeling

In the case study the *users* are the *citizens*, *company employees*, and *tax officers*. In the interaction points, we only need to concern ourselves with the type of the information that is exchanged, knowing that a default UI is automatically generated, and, equally important, it can always be customized without altering the task structure (Sect. 3.4). The *application tasks* are the automatic check whether an application is valid and taking care of filing the dossiers, decisions, and payments. The *coordination* involves parallelism between the applicant and company employees, and timing constraints as dossiers need to be completed within three months, and reminders need to be emitted after two months. To complicate things further, applicants can cancel requests, companies can decide not to provide the evidence, and applicants can resubmit rejected requests. Nevertheless, the top level task requestSolarPanelCompensation (Fig. 9a) can be structured by three subsequent steps: the application automatically checks whether the citizen meets the conditions (checkConditions); the declarations are obtained from the citizen and the roofing company (obtainDeclarations); the request is submitted and verified by a tax officer (submitOrCancelSubsidy). Although the task specification fits in about 200 loc, it is still too large for this paper. We discuss in more detail tasks checkConditions (Fig. 9b), obtainDeclarations (Fig. 9c), and submitOrCancelSubsidy (Fig. 10b).

Task checkConditions accesses several SDSs to assess whether the applicant is entitled to apply for the subsidy (owns the real estate and has not received subsidy in the past five years). In obtainDeclarations, the applicant provides the information regarding the installation of the solar panels (declarationApplicant), and, at the same time (-&&-), the roofing company provides the evidence that they have installed the solar panels (declarationCompany). (Figure 4 defines maybeCancel and deadlineWith.) The progress of this task is reported as a Declarations value, and is created by the pure function toDeclarations. It yields CanceledByCitizen if the applicant hit the 'panic' button, CanceledByCompany if the company decided not to provide information, and Declarations if all information has been provided.

The applicant (Fig. 9d) provides a TaxCompensationDocuments value (module Compensation.UoD, Fig. 7). Figure 12 shows the initial UI (left) that is generated for the enterInformation task, the specialized Date UI (middle), and manipulating a list of documents (right). At the same time, a parallel task (-||) is started that sends a reminder after two months if the first one has not been finished.

Before the company can be asked to provide the evidence, the applicant tells which roofing company has been involved (Fig. 10a). This choice involves the companiesOfType SDS (module ChamberOfCommerce.SDS, Fig. 8). The company receives (@:) the provideDeclaration task to provide the evidence (Fig. 11a).

When in possession of the required documents, the applicant can decide to submit the subsidy request to the tax authority in the submitOrCancelSubsidy task (Fig. 10b). If she submits the request, a tax authority employee with role "officer" can work on the processRequest task and decide whether or not to accept and further process the request. If the request is not approved, the applicant can check the reason and try to resubmit the request after editing it (resubmitSubsidy) or just cancel it entirely. If the request has been approved, the applicant terminates the entire procedure via the action labeled with *Continue*.

```
requestSolarPanelCompensation :: Citizen -> Task ()
requestSolarPanelCompensation citizen
    =           checkConditions citizen
    >>- \checks -> if (not checks.ownsRealEstate || not checks.noSubsidyPast5Years)
                     (showChecks checks)
    (               obtainDeclarations citizen
    >>- \result ->
    case result of
      CanceledByCitizen _ = return ()
      CanceledByCompany _ = showChecks {checks & declarationCompany = False}
      Declarations dossier = submitOrCancelSubsidy dossier)
where showChecks c = viewInformation msg [] c >>| return ()
      msg = "Your request can not be submitted; it does not satisfy these rules:"
```

(a) The top level task description of applying for compensation

```
checkConditions :: Citizen -> Task ValidityChecks
checkConditions applicant
    =           get currentDate
    >>- \today  -> get (currentRealEstate applicant)
    >>- \owns   -> get (currentDecisions  applicant.ssn ((==) Approved)
                                      (shiftDate (Years -5) today))
    >>- \grants -> return {ownsRealEstate      = any (\own -> own.isHomeAddress) owns
                          ,noSubsidyPast5Years = isEmpty grants
                          ,declarationCompany  = False}
```

(b) Checking the conditions of an applicant

```
:: Declarations = CanceledByCitizen NameHomeAddress
                | CanceledByCompany Company
                | Declarations       TaxSolarPanelDossier

obtainDeclarations :: Citizen -> Task Declarations
obtainDeclarations citizen
    =       get currentDate
    >>- \d -> deadlineWith (clientDeadlineDate d) Nothing
              (maybeCancel "Cancel Request"
              (declarationApplicant d -&&- declarationCompany d applicant))
    @ toDeclarations d applicant
where applicant = nameHomeAddressFromCitizen citizen
```

(c) The top level structure of obtaining applicant and company declarations

```
declarationApplicant :: Date -> Task TaxCompensationDocuments
declarationApplicant today
    = (enterInformation msg [] >>= return) -||
      (reminder (clientReminderDate today) "finish your request for tax compensation")
where
  msg = "Please enter the following information for your tax compensation request:"
```

(d) The applicant creates the solar panel tax compensation documents

Fig. 9. Task Modeling, part 1

```
declarationCompany:: Date NameHomeAddress -> Task (Company,Maybe CompanyDeclaration)
declarationCompany today applicant
  =   selectOfficialSolarPanelCompany
  >>- \company ->
        (UserWithId company.cocNo,"Request declaration")
        @: (provideDeclaration today applicant company)
              -||
          (reminder (clientReminderDate today) "finish the proof")
  >>= \decl -> viewInformation (msg_decision company decl) [] decl
  >>| return (company,decl)
where
  msg_decision c d = "Declaration was " +++ if (isNothing d) "negative" "positive"

selectOfficialSolarPanelCompany :: Task Company
selectOfficialSolarPanelCompany
  = enterChoiceWithShared msg [] (companiesOfType "solar panel company") >>= return
where
  msg = "Please enter the name of the company that installed the solar panels"
```

(a) The applicant identifies the roofing company

```
submitOrCancelSubsidy :: TaxSolarPanelDossier -> Task ()
submitOrCancelSubsidy dossier
  = viewInformation "You can submit the subsidy" [] dossier
  >>* [ OnAction (Action "Submit") (always (submitSubsidy dossier))
      , OnAction (Action "Cancel") (always (return ())) ]

submitSubsidy :: TaxSolarPanelDossier -> Task ()
submitSubsidy dossier
  =   get currentDate
  >>- \date -> let dossier = {dossier & date = date}
    in (( viewInformation "Your request is being processed" [] ())
          ||-
        ( (UserWithRole "officer","Subsidy request") @: processRequest dossier))
    >>- \decision -> viewInformation "Your request has been processed" [] decision
    >>* [ OnAction (Action "Edit request")    (ifCond (decision.status <> Approved)
                                                      (resubmitSubsidy dossier))
        , OnAction (Action "Cancel request") (ifCond (decision.status <> Approved)
                                                      (return ()))
        , OnAction (Action "Continue")       (ifCond (decision.status == Approved)
                                                      (return ())) ]
    >>| return ()

resubmitSubsidy :: TaxSolarPanelDossier -> Task ()
resubmitSubsidy dossier
  =           updateInformation "Edit your documents" [] dossier.request.documents
  >>= \new -> submitOrCancelSubsidy {dossier & request.documents = new }
```

(b) The applicant can submit, cancel, or update and resubmit a request

Fig. 10. Task Modeling, part 2

```
provideDeclaration:: Date NameHomeAddress Company -> Task (Maybe CompanyDeclaration)
provideDeclaration today applicant company
  = viewInformation msg [] applicant
    >>* [ OnAction (Action "Yes,⎵I⎵provide⎵declaration")
                              (always (provide today >>- return o Just))
        , OnAction (Action "No,⎵unknown⎵customer") (always (return Nothing))]
where
  msg = "This⎵customer⎵would⎵like⎵to⎵receive⎵a⎵declaration⎵for⎵the⎵tax⎵authorities:"

provide :: Date -> Task CompanyDeclaration
provide today
 = enterChoiceWithShared "Which⎵solar⎵panels⎵were⎵used?" [] acceptedSolarPanels
      -&&-
   enterInformation ("How⎵many⎵square⎵metres⎵of⎵solar⎵panels⎵have⎵been⎵installed?"
                     +++ "⎵[round⎵up⎵to⎵whole⎵numbers]") []
    -&&-
   enterInformation "Upload⎵photos" []
   >>= \(type,(area,photos)) -> return { solarPanelType  = type
                                       , roofPhotos      = photos
                                       , date            = today
                                       , roofAreaCovered = area }
```

(a) The roofing company is asked to provide evidence

```
processRequest :: TaxSolarPanelDossier -> Task Decision
processRequest dossier
=       viewInformation "Dossier⎵Request⎵Solar⎵Panel⎵Subsidy" [] dossier
          ||-
        updateInformation "Approve⎵or⎵explain⎵why⎵request⎵is⎵rejected:" [] Approved
  >>= \verdict -> get currentDate
  >>- \today   ->
  let invoice      = dossier.request.documents.invoiceAmount
      compensation = if (verdict == Approved)
                        (solar_panel_subsidy_law today.year invoice) 0
      decision     = { ssn            = dossier.request.ssn
                     , date           = today
                     , description    = "Solar⎵Panel⎵Subsidy⎵Request"
                     , status         = verdict
                     , invoiceAmount  = invoice
                     , compensation   = compensation }
      collection   = { ssn            = dossier.request.ssn
                     , description    = "Solar⎵Panel⎵Subsidy⎵Collection"
                     , date           = today
                     , amount         = compensation }
    in    viewInformation "Decision" [] decision
      >>| upd (append dossier) solarPanelSubsidyRequests
      >>| upd (append decision) decisions
      >>| upd (append collection)
              (if (amount < 0) collectionClaims collectionPayments)
      >>| return decision
```

(b) Tax officer decision and storage

Fig. 11. Task Modeling, part 3

Fig. 12. Default UI of the `declarationApplicant` task

3.4 UI Modeling

We illustrate this phase by means of the `provideDeclaration` task (Fig. 11a). The left image in Fig. 13 shows the default UI of this task. This is a rendering of the record structure of the type `NameHomeAddress`. If we write a function `customer ::` `NameHomeAddress -> String` that shows the same information in a single line of text, then, only by replacing the `[]` of the `viewInformation` task with `[ViewAs customer]`, we obtain the UI that is displayed in Fig. 13 in the middle image. If we prefer to use an image, and write the function `card` (Fig. 14), then, by replacing the `[]` of the `viewInformation` task with `[ViewUsing id (withImg card)]`, we obtain the UI that is displayed in Fig. 13 in the right image.

Fig. 13. Customizing the UI of the `provideDeclaration` task

```
card :: (ImageTag,*ImageTag) NameHomeAddress -> Image NameHomeAddress
card (t,ut) {name={forename,surname}, homeAddress={postcode,houseNumber}}
 = overlay [(AtMiddleX,AtMiddleY)] [] [tag ut
   (grid (Rows 2) (RowMajor,LeftToRight,TopToBottom)
      (repeat (AtLeft,AtMiddleY)) []
      [person, text font (foldr (+++) "" [forename, "␣", surname])
      ,house,  text font (foldr (+++) "" [postcode, "␣", toString houseNumber])]
      NoHost)]
   (Host (rect (imagexspan t *. 1.2) (imageyspan t *. 1.2) <@< {fill=white}))
where font = normalFontDef "Arial" 12.0
```

Fig. 14. Custom rendering of `NameHomeAddress` as an `Image`

3.5   Discussion

The case study supports the claim that TOSD achieves separation of concerns.

First, the type driven approach of TOP eliminates the need to deal with (G)UI construction, data (de)serialization, and code distribution. In the case study there is no code for these issues, yet it contains sufficient information to create a distributed, multi-user, web application.

Second, the modeling phases of TOSD have clearly formulated purposes. This helps the stakeholders and task engineers to determine which modeling phase to enter, what they should think about, and what they should not think about. In UoD Modeling, the entities and relations are determined without considering their rendering, serialization, and storage. In SDS Modeling, the shared information is identified, without considering by who, what, when, or where, it is used. In Task Modeling, the user (role)s and tasks are identified, without worrying how (G)UI's are created, how SDSs are accessed, or how work is distributed. In UI Modeling, any interaction point can be customized locally, without impacting the task structures, used SDSs, and UoD elements. One example of this in the case study is formed by the UoD entities Citizen, CadastreRealEstate, and OwnedRealEstate (Fig. 6), that are used in the relation realEstatesOfCitizen (Fig. 7), which, in turn, is used in the derived SDS currentRealEstate (Fig. 8), which, in turn, is used in the task checkConditions (Fig. 9b).

Third, the example also demonstrates that despite being created in separate modeling phases, entities can mutually strengthen each other. UoD entities can be stored and retrieved, viewed and manipulated in interaction points, and have a customized rendering. SDSs can be combined with any other, behave as a task, and be viewed and manipulated in interaction points, with a customized rendering. Tasks only need to define their own behaviour, knowing that their task value is the interface to other tasks and task combinators to obtain the proper progress of the application. The UI modeling can use UoD entities to customize the automatically created UI of the interaction points.

The separation of concerns leads to a modular structure of the source code and results in a short development time. The first version of the case study was created by a single person in two days. An additional day was used to translate it from Dutch to English and do some refactoring. The source code is small (817 loc, including empty and comment lines). The two largest modules contain the UoD modules that were presented in Sect. 3.1 (260 loc, 32%) and the tax authority tasks that were mostly presented in Sects. 3.3 and 3.4 (235 loc, 29%). The modules covering all the SDS's (Sect. 3.2) are small because most of them merely declare a SDS of a type (66 loc, 8%). One module contains generally useful task extensions to manipulate SDS's interactively (89 loc, 11%). One module deals with the payments, and viewing the status of citizens (86 loc, 11%). The resulting system allows users to play different roles and manipulate all SDS's. For the latter purpose it suffices to merely connect an interaction task with a SDS (21 loc, 2%). Finally, all top level tasks are collected and published as a single web application in the main module (60 loc, 7%).

4   Related Work

Functional Reactive Programming (FRP) was first introduced by Elliott and Hudak [13]. FRP has two central notions: *behaviours* and *events*. Behaviours are values that change continuously over time. Events are discrete. They can be real-world events, like a mouse click, or something more abstract like a predicate. Time-dependent behaviour is included in iTask by means of a SDS that provides access to the current time (similar to the SDS that provides access to the current date). This SDS can be turned into a task with watch (Fig. 2), and its evolving time value can be transformed via a function with @ (Fig. 3). Vice versa, sources of information (read-only SDS in TOP) are available in FRP, such as the mouseSF signal transformer of Fruit [7] that gives access to the current mouse position. The only other FRP state is obtained via a loop, resulting in state that is locally encapsulated within a signal transformer. The TOP SDS concept is more general than the state concept in FRP. TOP interaction points can be compared to a signal transformer in FRP of the same input and output type, except that in TOP the UI is generated automatically from the type, and the fact that interaction points can be coupled with SDS's. In FRP the signal transformers are tightly coupled with the types of their input and output and the programmer must use combinator functions to 'pipeline' the proper information to along the circuit. The iData framework [1,22] shares this feature with FRP. In TOP the coupling is much looser. In our experience with these systems we think that the TOP approach is better suited to achieve separation of concerns.

Elm [8] was initially promoted as a practical implementation of FRP. Recently, they abandoned FRP in favour of subscriptions. WebSharper [6,14] is another example of a reactive web framework. It offers a more traditional Model-View-Controller [17] (MVC) style framework for web application programming, whereas TOP operates at the higher abstraction level of tasks. MVC is a popular approach for implementing separation of concerns. The views concern the presentation layer, and part of the business layer is split between the model (keep the information consistent, regardless of how many, and which views exist on that information) and controller (that coordinates view changes to the model and vice versa). In TOP the interaction points are an extreme take on MVC because of the type-driven model based software development approach: the type of a model (entities and relations) suffices to automatically generate the views and controllers. Only when customizing a view, a 'controller' is defined explicitly (Sect. 2.4). Note that the TOP interaction points are typically only a small part of the business layer. The coordination of tasks and users and sharing information between them is dealt with via the task structure.

5   Conclusions

We have shown a systematic approach, called TOSD, to develop TOP programs in a way that results in a high degree of separation of concerns. This is obtained by identifying four development phases that each have a clearly stated concern and purpose. TOP supports each concern via the typed abstractions SDS, Task, and UI customization. These typed abstractions use the developed UoD entities and their functional relations as input.

Acknowledgements. This research is funded by the Royal Netherlands Navy and TNO. We thank the anonymous reviewers for their constructive comments.

References

1. Achten, P., Eekelen, M., Mol, M., Plasmeijer, R.: EditorArrow: an arrow-based model for editor-based programming. J. Funct. Program. **23**, 185–224 (2013)
2. Achten, P.: Why functional programming matters to me. In: Achten, P., Koopman, P. (eds.) The Beauty of Functional Code. LNCS, vol. 8106, pp. 79–96. Springer, Heidelberg (2013). https://doi.org/10.1007/978-3-642-40355-2_7
3. Achten, P., Stutterheim, J., Domoszlai, L., Plasmeijer, R.: Task oriented programming with purely compositional interactive scalable vector graphics. In: Tobin-Hochstadt, S. (ed.) Proceedings of the 26th 2014 International Symposium on Implementation and Application of Functional Languages, IFL 2014, pp. 7:1–7:13. ACM, New York (2014)
4. Achten, P., Stutterheim, J., Lijnse, B., Plasmeijer, R.: Towards the layout of things. In: Schrijvers, T. (ed.) Proceedings 28th International Symposium Implementation and Application of Functional Languages, IFL 2016. ACM, Leuven (2016)
5. Alimarine, A., Plasmeijer, R.: A generic programming extension for clean. In: Arts, T., Mohnen, M. (eds.) IFL 2001. LNCS, vol. 2312, pp. 168–185. Springer, Heidelberg (2002). https://doi.org/10.1007/3-540-46028-4_11
6. Bjornson, J., Tayanovskyy, A., Granicz, A.: Composing reactive GUIs in F# using WebSharper. In: Hage, J., Morazán, M.T. (eds.) IFL 2010. LNCS, vol. 6647, pp. 203–216. Springer, Heidelberg (2011). https://doi.org/10.1007/978-3-642-24276-2_13
7. Courtney, A.A.: Modeling user interfaces in a functional language. Ph.D. thesis, Yale University, USA, May 2004
8. Czaplicki, E., Chong, S.: Asynchronous functional reactive programming for GUIs. In: Proceedings of the 34th ACM SIGPLAN Conference on Programming Language Design and Implementation, PLDI 2013, pp. 411–422. ACM (2013)
9. Dahlström, E., Dengler, P., Grasso, A., Lilley, C., McCormack, C., Schepers, D., Watt, J.: Scalable vector graphics (SVG) 1.1, 2nd edn. Technical report, REC-SVG11-20110816, W3C Recommendation, 16 August 2011
10. Dijkstra, E.W.: Selected Writings on Computing: A Personal Perspective. Springer, New York (1982). https://doi.org/10.1007/978-1-4612-5695-3
11. Domoszlai, L., Lijnse, B., Plasmeijer, R.: Editlets: Type-based, client-side editors for iTasks. In: Tobin-Hochstadt, S. (ed.) Proceedings of the 26th 2014 International Symposium on Implementation and Application of Functional Languages, IFL 2014, pp. 6:1–6:13. ACM, New York (2014)
12. Domoszlai, L., Lijnse, B., Plasmeijer, R.: Parametric lenses: change notification for bidirectional lenses. In: Proceedings of the 26th 2014 International Symposium on Implementation and Application of Functional Languages, IFL 2014, pp. 9:1–9:11. ACM, New York (2014)
13. Elliott, C., Hudak, P.: Functional reactive animation. In: International Conference on Functional Programming (1997). http://conal.net/papers/icfp97/

14. Fowler, S., Denuzière, L., Granicz, A.: Reactive single-page applications with dynamic dataflow. In: Pontelli, E., Son, T.C. (eds.) PADL 2015. LNCS, vol. 9131, pp. 58–73. Springer, Cham (2015). https://doi.org/10.1007/978-3-319-19686-2_5
15. Hinze, R.: A new approach to generic functional programming. In: Reps, T. (ed.) Proceedings of the 27th International Symposium on Principles of Programming Languages, POPL 2000, Boston, MA, USA, pp. 119–132. ACM Press (2000)
16. Koopman, P., Plasmeijer, R.: A shallow embedded type safe extendable DSL for the Arduino. In: Serrano, M., Hage, J. (eds.) TFP 2015. LNCS, vol. 9547, pp. 104–123. Springer, Cham (2016). https://doi.org/10.1007/978-3-319-39110-6_6
17. Krasner, G.E., Pope, S.T.: A cookbook for using the model-view controller user interface paradigm in smalltalk-80. J. Object Oriented Program. 1(3), 26–49 (1988). http://dl.acm.org/citation.cfm?id=50757.50759
18. Lijnse, B., Jansen, J., Nanne, R., Plasmeijer, R.: Capturing the Netherlands coast guard's SAR workflow with iTasks. In: Proceedings of the 8th International ISCRAM Conference - Lisbon, Portugal, May 2011, pp. 1–10. National Civil Engineering Laboratory, Lisbon (2011)
19. Lijnse, B.: TOP to the rescue - task-oriented programming for incident response applications. Ph.D. thesis, Institute for Computing and Information Sciences, Radboud University Nijmegen, The Netherlands (2013). ISBN 978-90-820259-0-3
20. Lijnse, B., Jansen, J., Plasmeijer, R.: Incidone: a task-oriented incident coordination tool. In: Rothkrantz, L., Ristvej, J., Franco, Z. (eds.) Proceedings of the 9th International Conference on Information Systems for Crisis Response and Management, ISCRAM 2012, Vancouver, Canada, April 2012
21. Piers, J.: Task-oriented programming for developing non-distributed interruptible embedded systems. Master's thesis, Institute for Computing and Information Sciences, Radboud University, August 2016
22. Plasmeijer, R., Achten, P.: iData for the world wide web – programming interconnected web forms. In: Hagiya, M., Wadler, P. (eds.) FLOPS 2006. LNCS, vol. 3945, pp. 242–258. Springer, Heidelberg (2006). https://doi.org/10.1007/11737414_17
23. Plasmeijer, M.J., Achten, P.M., Koopman, P.W.M.: iTasks: executable specifications of interactive work flow systems for the web. In: Proceedings of the 12th International Conference on Functional Programming, ICFP 2007, pp. 141–152. ACM Press, Freiburg, 1–3 October 2007
24. Plasmeijer, R., Lijnse, B., Michels, S., Achten, P., Koopman, P.: Task-oriented programming in a pure functional language. In: Proceedings of the 2012 ACM SIGPLAN International Conference on Principles and Practice of Declarative Programming, PPDP 2012, pp. 195–206. ACM, Leuven, September 2012
25. Sommerville, I.: Software Engineering, 7th edn. Addison Wesley, Boston (2007)
26. Weelden, A.: Putting types to good use. Ph.D. thesis, Institute for Computing and Information Sciences, Radboud University Nijmegen, The Netherlands, 17 October 2007

Typed Relational Conversion

Petr Lozov[1], Andrei Vyatkin[1], and Dmitry Boulytchev[1,2]([⊠])

[1] St. Petersburg State University,
Universitetski pr., 28, 198504 St. Petersburg, Russia
lozov.peter@gmail.com, dewshick@gmail.com, dboulytchev@math.spbu.ru
[2] JetBrains Research, Universitetskaya emb., 7-9-11, bldg. 5A,
199034 St. Petersburg, Russia

Abstract. We address the problem of transforming typed functional programs into relational form. In this form, a program can be run in various "directions" with some arguments left free, making it possible to acquire different behaviors from a single specification. We specify the syntax, typing rules and semantics for the source language as well as its relational extension, describe the conversion and prove its correctness both in terms of typing and dynamic semantics. We also discuss the limitations of our approach, present the implementation of the conversion for the subset of OCaml and evaluate it on a number of realistic examples.

1 Introduction

Relational programming is an attractive technique, based on the idea of constructing programs as relations. While in general some relational effects can be reproduced with a number of languages for logic programming, such as Prolog, Mercury[1], or Curry[2], in a narrow sense relational programming amounts to writing relational specifications in miniKanren [10]. miniKanren[3], initially designed as a small relational DSL, embedded in Scheme/Racket, was later implemented for a number of general-purpose host languages, including Scala, Haskell, Standard ML and OCaml.

With relational approach, it becomes possible to give simple and elegant solutions for the problems, otherwise considered as tricky, tough, tedious, or boring [6]. For example, relational interpreters can be used to derive *quines*—programs, which reduce to themselves, as well as *twines* or *thrines* (pairs or triples of programs, reducing to each other) [8]; a straightforward relational description of simply typed lambda calculus [3] inference rules works both as type inferencer and inhabitation problem solver [5]; relational list sorting can be used to generate all permutations [13], etc.

On the other hand, writing relational specifications can sometimes be a tricky and error-prone task. Fortunately, many specifications can be written systematically by "generalizing" a certain functional program. From the very beginning,

---

[1] https://mercurylang.org.
[2] http://www-ps.informatik.uni-kiel.de/currywiki.
[3] http://minikanren.org.

© Springer International Publishing AG, part of Springer Nature 2018
M. Wang and S. Owens (Eds.): TFP 2017, LNCS 10788, pp. 39–58, 2018.
https://doi.org/10.1007/978-3-319-89719-6_3

the conversion from functional to relational form was considered as an element of relational programming thesaurus [10]. However, the traditional approach—*unnesting*—was formulated for an untyped case, worked only for specifically written programs and was never implemented.

We present a generalized form of relational conversion, which can be applied to typed terms in general form. We study the relational conversion for a small ML-like language (essentially, a certain subset of OCaml), equipped with Hindley-Milner type system with let-polymorphism [15]. We start from retelling the syntax, typing rules, and operational semantics, and then extend the source language with a conventional set of relational constructs. This set corresponds to existing typed embedding of miniKanren into OCaml [13]. We then present typing rules and develop operational semantics for this relational extension; to our knowledge, this is the first attempt to specify formal semantics for miniKanren. Next, we develop formal rules for relational conversion and prove, that these rules respect both typing and semantics. Finally, we describe the implementation of a relational converter and demonstrate its application for a number of problems, for some of which we present a relational solution for the first time.

We would like to express our gratitude to William Byrd and the anonymous reviewers for their constructive remarks, which, we believe, led to the improvement of the presentation.

2   Relational Programming in miniKanren

In the context of this paper, we will use a certain concrete implementation of miniKanren—a shallow DSL for OCaml[4], called OCanren [13]. OCanren corresponds to miniKanren with disequality constraints [1], and (modulo typing) follows the original implementation [11,12]. Here we describe the external view on OCanren, giving the only intuitive meaning of its constructs; the formal description will be presented in Sect. 3.2. We also use a simplified syntax, which is a little bit different from the concrete syntax in actual implementation, but assumed to be easier to read.

The central notion of miniKanren is *goal*; in OCanren a goal can be an arbitrary expression of reserved goal type, which we denote $\mho$. There are only five syntactic forms of goals (denoted below as g, g_1, g_2, etc.):

- conjunction $g_1 \wedge g_2$;
- disjunction $g_1 \vee g_2$;
- fresh variable introduction **fresh** $(x)\ g$;
- unification $t_1 \equiv t_2$;
- disequality constraint $t_1 \not\equiv t_2$.

Two last forms of goals constitute a basis for goal construction; here t_1 and t_2 are *terms*. In OCanren a term is an arbitrary expression of polymorphic logic

---

[4] https://github.com/dboulytchev/ocanren.

type α^o. The postfix notation $\square^o$ is a traditional way to denote relational entities, and we will use it for types as well[5].

The simplest expression of logic type is a variable, bound in **fresh**. Another example is a primitive value, *injected* into the logic domain with a built-in primitive "↑", such as ↑ 3 (of type `int`^{o}) or ↑**true** (of type `bool`^{o}). Other types (pairs, lists, user-defined algebraic datatypes, etc.) can be used in relational specifications as well, being injected by the same primitive. For example, expression ↑ (1," abc ") has the type (int * string)^o, ↑ [1; 2; 3]—the type (int list)^o, etc. The subtle part is that (since the unification only works for logical types) the placement of "^{o}" determines the granularity of unification. Indeed, a logical variable can only be placed where logical type is expected. Thus, in unification one can use a value of type (int * int)^o as *a whole*, but in order to control the *contents* of the pair relationally, the type (int^o, int^o)^o is required. This makes it impossible to reuse some built-in or standard types in relational code—for example, predefined list type is not flexible enough, since it does not allow the tail of the list to be logical. Instead, logical list type has to be introduced:

type α llist = Nil | Cons **of** α^o * (α llist)^o

With logical list type, we can implement some relations for lists:

val append : (α llist)^o → (α llist)^o → (α llist)^o → Ⓖ
let rec append^o x y xy =
  (x ≡ ↑Nil ∧ xy ≡ y) ∨
  (**fresh** (h t ty)
    x ≡ ↑(Cons (h, t)) ∧
    xy ≡ ↑(Cons (h, ty)) ∧
    append^o t y ty
)

Here we defined relational list concatenation **append**^{o}, a canonical example in the field. This ternary relation is constructed, using case analysis and recursion:

1. If the first list is empty, then the second and the third lists must be equal.
2. Otherwise, the first list can be split into a head and a tail, and two fresh variables h and t are needed to denote them. We also need a fresh variable ty to denote the list, such that appending y to t equals ty. To ensure this property, we use a recursive call to **append**^{o}. Finally, we acquire the final result by consing h and ty.

The definition of **append**^{o} takes three logical lists x, y and xy as arguments, and constructs a goal, which can be executed or combined with other goals. In the former case, a stream of *answers* is returned. An element of the stream

---

[5] In the real implementation the terms have a more complex two-parametric type, which encodes a tagging, needed to be performed when the results of the relational program are returned into the functional world; these details, however, are irrelevant to the objectives of the paper, and we stick with the simplified version.

contains the description of certain constraints for logical variables, which have to be respected in order for the relation to hold. We denote the running primitive "⤳", so

> **fresh** (q) append^o ↑(Cons (↑1, ↑Nil)) q ↑Nil ⤳ []

returns an empty stream, since there is no list q, such that appending Cons (1, Nil) and q gives empty list, while

> **fresh** (q) append^o q ↑Nil ↑(Cons (↑1, ↑Nil)) ⤳ [q ↦ Cons (1, Nil)]

discovers the expected constraint for the variable q.

As it can be seen from the type, relational concatenation is polymorphic, like its functional counterpart. However, the query

> append^o ↑(Cons (↑λx.x, ↑Nil)) q ↑(Cons (↑λy.y, ↑Nil))

ends with a run-time error due to inability to unify closures. This is a fundamental limitation in original miniKanren as well, as it deals only with first-order syntactic unification [2]. This example demonstrates, that, unlike pure OCaml, the typing in OCanren is somewhat weak. In order to restore the strong typing, some of the type variables have to be bounded to range over only non-functional types. The lack of direct support for bounded polymorphism [9] in OCaml makes this step problematic. Our experience, however, shows, that in practice this deficiency rarely gets in the way. In the following development, we assume, that in polymorphic types some type variables may be implicitly bounded by the set of non-function types, and these boundings are respected in all instantiations of those type variables.

Finally, we describe the unnesting technique [10], which was introduced as a method for manual transformation of functional programs into relational form. Unnesting introduces a new name for each nested subexpression; now, when the value of each subexpression is bound to a certain variable, the conversion is straightforward: each pattern-matching construct is transformed into a disjunction, new names, introduced in pattern bindings and unnestings, are transformed into **fresh** variables, and each converted function is supplied with the additional argument, unified with the result. As a result we consider, again, the list concatenation function (see Fig. 1a). The result of unnesting is shown on Fig. 1b, while the final relational form—on Fig. 1c.

However, not every definition can be converted to a relational form by unnesting. Consider, for example, the definition on Fig. 2a. Unnesting would transform this program into the form, shown on Fig. 2b, which is obviously invalid, since it unifies a function f with a logical variable r. In order to apply unnesting, one needs to η-expand the definition of g, making the functional nature of its return type syntactically visible. We stress, that relational conversion, described in Sect. 4, is essentially different from unnesting. In particular, we use η-expansion in a very limited manner (only in one case).

```
let rec append x y =          let rec append x y =
  match x with                  match x with
  | Nil → y                     | Nil → y
  | Cons (h, t) →               | Cons (h, t) →
      Cons (h, append t y)          let ty = append t y in
                                     Cons (h, ty)
            (a)                             (b)
               let rec appendᵒ x y xy =
                 (t ≡ ↑Nil ∧ xy ≡ y) ∨
                 (fresh (h t ty)
                   (x  ≡ ↑Cons (h, t)) ∧
                   (xy ≡ ↑Cons (h, ty)) ∧
                   (appendᵒ t y ty)
               )
                            (c)
```

Fig. 1. Unnesting example

```
let bar y =                   let barᵒ y r =
  let f x = x in                let f x r = x ≡ r in
  let g a = f in                let g a r = f ≡ r in
  g A y                         g ↑A y r
            (a)                             (b)
```

Fig. 2. Unnesting: invalid case

3   The Source Language and Relational Extension

Our development of relational conversion is based on the idea of transforming a program in a functional language into a program in *relational extension* of that language. In the context of miniKanren, this approach looks quite natural, since miniKanren itself, as a DSL, reuses many important features (for example, function definitions) from a host language.

In this section, we present a formal description of a small functional language, taken as a source for relational conversion. We describe its syntax, typing rules, and semantics, and then extend it with relational constructs. We specify the typing rules and semantics for the extension as well.

3.1   The Source Language

The syntax of our source functional language is shown on Fig. 3. It consists of a lambda calculus, enriched with constructors with fixed arities C^n, patterns p and pattern-matching constructs, and expressions for recursive/non-recursive let-bindings. Among the constructors we distinguish two nullary interpreted constructors **true** and **false**, and add a boolean equality operator "=".

In a pattern matching, we only allow shallow patterns (which is not an essential limitation) and do not allow wildcards (which is important—converting wildcard pattern matching into relational form would require essentially different projections).

Our language is equipped with Hindley-Milner type system, and we present the typing rules in a conventional syntax-directed form on Fig. 4. Besides type variables and function types, our system contains a number of implicitly defined algebraic datatypes T^k, and we stipulate, that each constructor C^n belongs to the exactly one datatype. In the rule CONSTR$_T$, we assume that type t^C has the form $T^k(t_1, \ldots, t_k)$, where each of the types t_i is recovered from the types t_i^C of arguments of constructor C^n and, moreover, these types agree in the sense of constructor application. Similarly, in the rule MATCH$_T$, the types of all $C_i^{k_i}(x_1^i, \ldots, x_{k_i}^i)$ are expected to be equal t^C, and $t_j^{C_i}$ is a type of j-th argument of constructor C_i, used in the pattern. The rule EQ$_T$ specifies that both operands of equality operator must have the same (but arbitrary) type. Thus, we can call this operator "polymorphic equality" (Fig. 5).

$$\mathcal{E} = x$$
$$\lambda x.e$$
$$e_1\ e_2$$
$$C^n(e_1, \ldots, e_n)$$
$$\underline{\text{true}}$$
$$\underline{\text{false}}$$
$$\underline{\text{let}}\ x = e_1\ \underline{\text{in}}\ e_2$$
$$\underline{\text{let}}\ \underline{\text{rec}}\ f = \lambda x.e_1\ \underline{\text{in}}\ e_2$$
$$e_1 = e_2$$
$$\underline{\text{match}}\ e\ \underline{\text{with}}\ \{p_i \rightarrow e_i\}$$

$$\mathcal{P} = C^n(x_1, \ldots, x_n)$$

Fig. 3. The syntax of source language

Types:

$$\mathcal{X} = \alpha, \beta, \ldots \qquad \text{(type variables)}$$
$$\mathcal{D} = \textbf{bool}, T^n, \ldots \qquad \text{(datatype constructors)}$$
$$\mathcal{T} = \alpha \mid T^k(t_1, \ldots, t_k) \mid t_1 \rightarrow t_2\ \text{(types)}$$
$$\mathcal{S} = \forall \bar{\alpha}.t \qquad \text{(type schemas)}$$

Typing rules:

$$\Gamma \vdash \underline{\text{true}}, \underline{\text{false}} : \textbf{bool} \qquad [\text{BOOL}_T]$$

$$\frac{\Gamma \vdash e_1 : t \quad \Gamma \vdash e_2 : t}{\Gamma \vdash e_1 = e_2 : \textbf{bool}} \qquad [\text{EQ}_T]$$

$$\frac{\Gamma \vdash e_i : t_i^C}{\Gamma \vdash C^n(e_1, \ldots, e_n) : t^C} \qquad [\text{CONSTR}_T]$$

$$\Gamma, x : \forall \bar{\alpha}.t \vdash x : t[\bar{\alpha} \leftarrow \bar{t'}] \qquad [\text{VAR}_T]$$

$$\frac{\Gamma \vdash f : t_1 \rightarrow t_2 \quad \Gamma \vdash e : t_1}{\Gamma \vdash f\ e : t_2} \qquad [\text{APP}_T]$$

$$\frac{\Gamma, x : t_1 \vdash f : t_2}{\Gamma \vdash \lambda x.f : t_1 \rightarrow t_2} \qquad [\text{ABS}_T]$$

$$\frac{\Gamma \vdash e_1 : t_1 \quad \Gamma, x : \forall \bar{\alpha}.t_1 \vdash e_2 : t}{\Gamma \vdash \underline{\text{let}}\ x = e_1\ \underline{\text{in}}\ e_2 : t}, \ \bar{\alpha} = FV(t_1) \setminus FV(\Gamma) \qquad [\text{LET}_T]$$

$$\frac{\Gamma, f : t_1 \vdash \lambda x.e_1 : t_1 \quad \Gamma, f : \forall \bar{\alpha}.t_1 \vdash e_2 : t}{\Gamma \vdash \underline{\text{let}}\ \underline{\text{rec}}\ f = \lambda x.e_1\ \underline{\text{in}}\ e_2 : t}, \ \bar{\alpha} = FV(t_1) \setminus FV(\Gamma) \qquad [\text{LETREC}_T]$$

$$\frac{\Gamma \vdash e : t^C \quad \Gamma, x_1^i : t_1^{C_i}, \ldots, x_{k_i}^i : t_{k_i}^{C_i} \vdash e_i : t}{\Gamma \vdash \underline{\text{match}}\ e\ \underline{\text{with}}\ \{C_i^{k_i}(x_1^i, \ldots, x_{k_i}^i) \rightarrow e_i\} : t} \qquad [\text{MATCH}_T]$$

Fig. 4. Typing rules for the source language

Values:

$$\mathcal{V} = C^n(v_1, \ldots, v_n) \mid \lambda x.e \mid \mu f \lambda x.e \mid \underline{true} \mid \underline{false}$$

Contexts:

$$\mathcal{C} = \Box\, e \mid v\, \Box \mid \underline{let}\ x = \Box\ \underline{in}\ e \mid \underline{match}\ \Box\ \underline{with}\ \{p_i {\rightarrow} e_i\} \mid C^n(\bar{v}, \Box, \bar{e}) \mid \Box{=}e \mid v{=}\Box$$

Stack of contexts:

$$\mathcal{S} = \epsilon \mid \mathcal{C} : \mathcal{S}$$

States:

$\langle \mathcal{S}, e \rangle$ (stack of contexts, expression); $\langle \epsilon, e \rangle$ (initial state); $\langle \epsilon, v \rangle$ (final state)

Transitions:

$$\langle C : \mathcal{S},\, v \rangle \rightarrow \langle \mathcal{S},\, C[v] \rangle \qquad\qquad\qquad\qquad\qquad\text{[Value]}$$

$$\langle \mathcal{S},\, f\, e \rangle \rightarrow \langle \Box\, e : \mathcal{S},\, f \rangle \quad\text{[AppL]} \qquad\qquad \langle \mathcal{S},\, v\, e_2 \rangle \rightarrow \langle v\, \Box : \mathcal{S},\, e_2 \rangle \quad\text{[AppR]}$$

$$\langle \mathcal{S},\, e_1 = e_2 \rangle \rightarrow \langle \Box = e_2 : \mathcal{S},\, e_1 \rangle \quad\text{[EqL]} \qquad \langle \mathcal{S},\, v = e \rangle \rightarrow \langle v = \Box : \mathcal{S},\, e \rangle \quad\text{[EqR]}$$

$$\langle \mathcal{S},\, v = v \rangle \rightarrow \langle \mathcal{S},\, \underline{true} \rangle \qquad\qquad\qquad\qquad\qquad\text{[EqTrue]}$$

$$\langle \mathcal{S},\, v_1 = v_2 \rangle \rightarrow \langle \mathcal{S},\, \underline{false} \rangle,\ v_1 \neq v_2 \qquad\qquad\qquad\quad\text{[EqFalse]}$$

$$\langle \mathcal{S},\, (\lambda x.e)\, v \rangle \rightarrow \langle \mathcal{S},\, e[x \leftarrow v] \rangle \qquad\qquad\qquad\qquad\quad\text{[Beta]}$$

$$\langle \mathcal{S},\, (\mu f \lambda x.e)\, v \rangle \rightarrow \langle \mathcal{S},\, e[f \leftarrow \mu f \lambda x.e,\, x \leftarrow v] \rangle \qquad\qquad\text{[Mu]}$$

$$\langle \mathcal{S},\, C^n(v_1, \ldots, v_{k-1}, e_k, \ldots, e_n) \rangle \rightarrow \langle C^n(v_1, \ldots, v_{k-1}, \Box, \ldots, e_n) : \mathcal{S},\, e_k \rangle \quad\text{[Constr]}$$

$$\langle \mathcal{S},\, \underline{let}\ x = e_1\ \underline{in}\ e_2 \rangle \rightarrow \langle \underline{let}\ x = \Box\ \underline{in}\ e_2 : \mathcal{S},\, e_1 \rangle \qquad\qquad\text{[Let]}$$

$$\langle \mathcal{S},\, \underline{let}\ x = v\ \underline{in}\ e \rangle \rightarrow \langle \mathcal{S},\, e[x \leftarrow v] \rangle \qquad\qquad\qquad\text{[LetVal]}$$

$$\langle \mathcal{S},\, \underline{let}\ \underline{rec}\ f = \lambda x.e_1\ \underline{in}\ e_2 \rangle \rightarrow \langle \mathcal{S},\, e_2[f \leftarrow \mu f \lambda x.e_1] \rangle \qquad\text{[LetRec]}$$

$$\langle \mathcal{S},\, \underline{match}\ e\ \underline{with}\ \{p_i {\rightarrow} e_i\} \rangle \rightarrow \langle \underline{match}\ \Box\ \underline{with}\ \{p_i {\rightarrow} e_i\} : \mathcal{S},\, e \rangle \quad\text{[Match]}$$

$$\langle \mathcal{S},\, \underline{match}\ C_k^{n_k}(v_1, \ldots, v_{n_k})\ \underline{with}\ \{C_i^{n_i}(x_1^i, \ldots, x_{n_i}^i) \rightarrow e_i\} \rangle \rightarrow \langle \mathcal{S},\, e_k[x_j^k \leftarrow v_j] \rangle \quad\text{[MatchVal]}$$

Fig. 5. Semantics for the source language

We describe the semantics of our language in the form of transition system. The transition relation

$$\langle \mathcal{S}, e \rangle \rightarrow \langle \mathcal{S}', e' \rangle$$

describes a one step of evaluation of expression e with a stack of contexts $\mathcal{S}$, which results in a new stack $\mathcal{S}'$ and a new expression e'. A context is an expression with a unique hole; informally speaking, a stack of contexts describes a path in the expression being evaluated from the topmost construct to the point, where the evaluation currently is taking place. For a context C and an expression e, we denote by $C[e]$ a complete expression with no holes, which is obtained by plugging e into the unique hole of C. From each state $\langle C_1 : C_2 : \cdots : C_k, e \rangle$ we can build an expression $C_k[\ldots[C_2[C_1[e]]]\ldots]$, which represents an intermediate result of evaluation according to a small-step semantics. This form of semantic description originates from Felleisen-style [16] approach for small-step semantics, and we've chosen it since it can be naturally extended for a relational case.

Our semantics describes call-by-value left-to-right evaluation; in the rules BETA, MU, LETVAL, LETREC and MATCHVAL, we perform capture-avoiding substitutions, which respect the names in abstractions and let-bindings. In the rule MATCHVAL we assume, that at most one pattern matches the scrutinee— this is an important difference from the usual semantics of pattern matching, when the patterns are examined in a top-down manner until the matching succeeds. In the rules EQTRUE and EQFALSE we assume, that the values v, v_1, v_2 do not have the forms $\lambda x \ldots$ or $\mu f \ldots$.

Finally, for a closed expression e and a value v, we write $e \rightsquigarrow^f v$, iff

$$\langle \epsilon, e \rangle \rightarrow^* \langle \epsilon, v \rangle$$

where ϵ—an empty stack, and "$\rightarrow^*$" is a reflexive-transitive closure of "$\rightarrow$".

3.2 Relational Extension

The relational extension adds five conventional miniKanren expressions for constructing goals; the syntax is shown on Fig. 6. Since relational constructs are added to regular functional ones, it becomes possible to construct expressions like $\lambda x.(x \wedge \lambda y.y)$, etc. In order to rule such pathological expressions out, we devised an extension for the type system of the source language. In fact, this approach follows the actual implementation for OCaml, where a careful choice of types for representing terms and goals made it possible to reject the majority of non-well-formed programs at compile-time.

Our extension for the type system introduces one interpreted datatype constructor $\square^o$ with one data constructor $\uparrow$—a polymorphic type and a constructor for logical terms. In addition, we introduce an interpreted type of goals $\mathfrak{G}$, which is distinct from all other types. The typing rules for the relational extension are shown on Fig. 7. These rules describe rather expected typing: in unification and disequality constraints only terms of the same logical type can be used, and conjunction and disjunction can only be taken for goals. Note, in our extension a term can be calculated as a result of arbitrary expression in initial functional language (as long as this expression has expected logical type), but such "higher-order" terms will never appear as a result of relational conversion, so, in fact, relational extension we describe here defines a richer language, than we actually need.

The semantics of extended language is shown on Fig. 8. First, the state is extended: besides the stack of contexts and current expression it now contains a set of used *semantic variables* Σ and a *logical state* σ. Semantic variables are allocated and substituted for syntactic logic variable occurrences, when **fresh** expression is evaluated (see rule FRESH). Logical states are affected, when unification or disequality constraint is evaluated; we explain them in details below. All existing rules for the initial language are considered rewritten to propagate newly added components of states unchanged. Then, we modify the substitution to respect names, bound in **fresh** as well. Next, we consider two new kinds of values: a semantic variable and a special value **success**. The former is a result of evaluation for a free logic variable, the latter—the result of evaluation for a succeeded goal.

We also extend the definition of context to handle the new kinds of expressions. In unification and disequality constraint, the terms are evaluated left-to-right. Conjunction and disjunction, however, evaluate nondeterministically: in disjunction only one subgoal is chosen (see rules DISJL and DISJR), a conjunction can evaluate either left, or right subgoal first (see rules CONJSTARTL and CONJSTARTR). When chosen subgoal is evaluated to the value **success**, the other subgoal starts its evaluation (rules CONJL and CONJR). We have chosen a nondeterministic variant for the semantics, since different existing miniKanren implementations use (a little bit) different search, and we do not want to depend on the implementation details. An opposite side of this solution is that for a concrete program and a concrete miniKanren implementation, the result of the evaluation might not coincide with that, prescribed by the semantics: in some concrete implementation a program can diverge, while nondeterministic semantics may still define a certain scenario to complete with a result. We argue, that in this case, it will always be possible to rewrite a program or/and interpreter to converge according to that scenario.

$$\mathcal{E} \mathrel{+}= \underline{\text{fresh}}\ (x)\ e$$
$$e_1 \equiv e_2$$
$$e_1 \not\equiv e_2$$
$$e_1 \vee e_2$$
$$e_1 \wedge e_2$$

Fig. 6. The syntax of relational extension

Finally, we describe the structure of a logical state and the implementation of unification and disequality constraint. The development is mainly based on the existing implementation [1] and standard approaches for implementing unification [2,14]. We, therefore, assume the familiarity of the reader with the following notions:

- substitution (θ);
- application of substitution θ to a term t $(t\,\theta)$;
- composition of substitutions $(\theta\theta')$;
- most general unifier of two terms $(mgu\,(t_1, t_2))$.

A logical state contains two components

$$\sigma = (\theta, \Theta^-)$$

where θ is a substitution, Θ^-—a set of negative substitutions, describing disequality constraints, which can potentially be violated. The initial state contains undefined substitution and empty set:

$$\iota = (\bot, \varnothing)$$

The effect of unification is described by the following primitive:

$$\mathbf{unify}\,(\sigma, t_1, t_2) = \mathbf{unify}\,((\theta, \Theta^-), t_1, t_2)$$

First, it calculates the most general unifier for the terms under consideration w.r.t. current substitution:

$$\rho = mgu\,(t_1\,\theta, t_2\,\theta)$$

Types:

$$\mathcal{L} = \alpha^o \mid (T^n(l_1, \ldots, l_n))^o \ \text{(logical types)}$$
$$\mathcal{T} += \mathfrak{G}$$

Typing rules:

$$\frac{\Gamma, x : l \vdash e : \mathfrak{G}}{\Gamma \vdash \underline{\text{fresh}} \ (x) \ e : \mathfrak{G}} \qquad [\text{Fresh}_T]$$

$$\frac{\Gamma \vdash e_1 : l \quad \Gamma \vdash e_2 : l}{\Gamma \vdash e_1 \equiv e_2 : \mathfrak{G}} \quad [\text{Unify}_T] \qquad \frac{\Gamma \vdash e_1 : l \quad \Gamma \vdash e_2 : l}{\Gamma \vdash e_1 \not\equiv e_2 : \mathfrak{G}} \qquad [\text{Disequality}_T]$$

$$\frac{\Gamma \vdash e_1 : \mathfrak{G} \quad \Gamma \vdash e_2 : \mathfrak{G}}{\Gamma \vdash e_1 \wedge e_2 : \mathfrak{G}} \quad [\text{Conjunction}_T] \qquad \frac{\Gamma \vdash e_1 : \mathfrak{G} \quad \Gamma \vdash e_2 : \mathfrak{G}}{\Gamma \vdash e_1 \vee e_2 : \mathfrak{G}} \qquad [\text{Disjunction}_T]$$

Fig. 7. Typing rules for the relational extension

Semantic variables:

$$\mathfrak{S} = \mathfrak{s}_1, \mathfrak{s}_2, \ldots$$
$$\Sigma, \Sigma' \cdots \subset 2^S \ \text{(sets of allocated semantics variables)}$$
$$\langle \Sigma', \mathfrak{s} \rangle \leftarrow \underline{\text{new}} \ \Sigma, \ \Sigma' = \Sigma \cup \{\mathfrak{s}\}, \ \mathfrak{s} \notin \Sigma \ \text{(allocation of a new semantic variable)}$$

Values:

$$\mathcal{V} += \underline{\text{success}} \mid \mathfrak{s}$$

Contexts:

$$\mathcal{C} += \Box \equiv e \mid v \equiv \Box \mid \Box \not\equiv e \mid v \not\equiv \Box \mid \Box \wedge e \mid e \wedge \Box$$

States:

$$\langle \Sigma, \mathcal{S}, e, \sigma \rangle \ \text{(set of allocated semantic variables, stack of contexts, expression, logical state)}$$
$$\langle \varnothing, \epsilon, e, \iota \rangle \ \text{(initial state)}$$

Transitions:

$$\langle \Sigma, \mathcal{S}, \underline{\text{fresh}}(x) \ e, \sigma \rangle \rightsquigarrow \langle \Sigma', \mathcal{S}, e[x \leftarrow \mathfrak{s}], \sigma \rangle, \ \langle \Sigma', \mathfrak{s} \rangle \leftarrow \underline{\text{new}} \ \Sigma \qquad [\text{Fresh}]$$

$$\langle \Sigma, \mathcal{S}, e_1 \equiv e_2, \sigma \rangle \rightsquigarrow \langle \Sigma, \Box \equiv e_2 : \mathcal{S}, e_1, \sigma \rangle \qquad [\text{UnifyL}]$$

$$\langle \Sigma, \mathcal{S}, v \equiv e, \sigma \rangle \rightsquigarrow \langle \Sigma, v \equiv \Box : \mathcal{S}, e, \sigma \rangle \qquad [\text{UnifyR}]$$

$$\langle \Sigma, \mathcal{S}, v_1 \equiv v_2, \sigma \rangle \rightsquigarrow \langle \Sigma, \mathcal{S}, \underline{\text{success}}, \sigma' \rangle, \ \textbf{unify} \ (\sigma, v_1, v_2) = \sigma' \qquad [\text{Unify}]$$

$$\langle \Sigma, \mathcal{S}, e_1 \not\equiv e_2, \sigma \rangle \rightsquigarrow \langle \Sigma, \Box \not\equiv e_2 : \mathcal{S}, e_1, \sigma \rangle \qquad [\text{DisEqL}]$$

$$\langle \Sigma, \mathcal{S}, v \not\equiv e, \sigma \rangle \rightsquigarrow \langle \Sigma, v \not\equiv \Box : \mathcal{S}, e, \sigma \rangle \qquad [\text{DisEqR}]$$

$$\langle \Sigma, \mathcal{S}, v_1 \not\equiv v_2, \sigma \rangle \rightsquigarrow \langle \Sigma, \mathcal{S}, \underline{\text{success}}, \sigma' \rangle, \ \textbf{diseq} \ (\sigma, v_1, v_2) = \sigma' \qquad [\text{DisEq}]$$

$$\langle \Sigma, \mathcal{S}, e_1 \vee e_2, \sigma \rangle \rightsquigarrow \langle \Sigma, \mathcal{S}, e_1, \sigma \rangle \qquad [\text{DisjL}]$$

$$\langle \Sigma, \mathcal{S}, e_1 \vee e_2, \sigma \rangle \rightsquigarrow \langle \Sigma, \mathcal{S}, e_2, \sigma \rangle \qquad [\text{DisjR}]$$

$$\langle \Sigma, \mathcal{S}, e_1 \wedge e_2, \sigma \rangle \rightsquigarrow \langle \Sigma, \Box \wedge e_2 : \mathcal{S}, e_1, \sigma \rangle \qquad [\text{ConjStartL}]$$

$$\langle \Sigma, \mathcal{S}, e_1 \wedge e_2, \sigma \rangle \rightsquigarrow \langle \Sigma, e_1 \wedge \Box : \mathcal{S}, e_2, \sigma \rangle \qquad [\text{ConjStartR}]$$

$$\langle \Sigma, \mathcal{S}, \underline{\text{success}} \wedge e, \sigma \rangle \rightsquigarrow \langle \Sigma, \mathcal{S}, e, \sigma \rangle \qquad [\text{ConjL}]$$

$$\langle \Sigma, \mathcal{S}, e \wedge \underline{\text{success}}, \sigma \rangle \rightsquigarrow \langle \Sigma, \mathcal{S}, e, \sigma \rangle \qquad [\text{ConjR}]$$

Fig. 8. Semantics for the relational extension

If there is no such ρ, the unification fails, and the evaluation terminates unsuccessfully. Otherwise, ρ has to be checked against the disequality constraints, represented by Θ^- (if Θ^- is empty, the check succeeds immediately).

Being a substitution, ρ at the same time can be considered as the following unification problem: we can try to unify a pair of terms

$$t_l = (\mathfrak{s}_1, \ldots, \mathfrak{s}_k)$$
$$t_r = (\rho(\mathfrak{s}_1), \ldots, \rho(\mathfrak{s}_k))$$

where $\{\mathfrak{s}_i\} = dom(\rho)$. We pick every substitution $\theta^- \in \Theta^-$ and calculate the $mgu(t_l \theta^-, t_r \theta^-)$. There are three possible outcomes:

1. The unification fails. This means, that disequality constraint, represented by θ^-, can no longer be violated. We remove θ^- from Θ^- and continue with the next disequality constraint.
2. The unification succeeds with the empty substitution. This means, that disequality constraint, represented by θ^-, is violated. The check stops, and the whole top-level unification fails.
3. The unification succeeds with a non-empty substitution θ'^-. This means, that in order not to violate disequality constraint, represented by θ^-, θ'^- has to be respected. We replace θ^- with θ'^- in Θ^- and continue with the next disequality constraint.

If the disequality check succeeds, by the end we have a modified set Θ'^-, and we assume

$$\textbf{unify}\,((\theta, \Theta^-), t_1, t_2) = (\theta\rho, \Theta'^-)$$

The evaluation of disequality constraint is performed in a similar manner using the primitive

$$\textbf{diseq}\,(\sigma, t_1, t_2) = \textbf{diseq}\,((\theta, \Theta^-), t_1, t_2)$$

First, the $mgu(t_1 \theta, t_2 \theta)$ is calculated. Again, there are three possible cases:

1. The unification fails. This means, that disequality constraint is satisfied.
2. The unification succeeds with the empty substitution. This means, that disequality constraint is violated.
3. The unification succeeds with a non-empty substitution θ'^-. This means, that this substitution describes the disequality constraint, which has to be respected in the future, so we add it to Θ^-.

If disequality constraint succeeds, we obtain a (potentially) modified set Θ'^-, and we assume

$$\textbf{diseq}\,((\theta, \Theta^-), t_1, t_2) = (\theta, \Theta'^-)$$

Finally, for a closed goal g and a logical state σ, we define $g \leadsto^r \sigma$, iff

$$\langle \varnothing, \epsilon, g, \iota \rangle \leadsto^* \langle \Sigma, \epsilon, \underline{\text{success}}, \sigma \rangle \text{ for some } \Sigma$$

where "$\leadsto^*$" is a reflexive-transitive closure of "$\leadsto$".

One may notice, that the typing rules for the relational extension add nothing more than some interpreted types and symbols w.r.t. the type system of the substrate language. Thus, it is rather expected, that the relational extension inherits all its useful properties (like progress and type preservation). Surprisingly, this is not completely so. Indeed, the only value for goals is <u>success</u>, but, obviously, not every goal succeeds (for example, $A \equiv B$ always fails). Thus, our relational extension lacks the progress property—a decently typed non-value goal sometimes cannot make a step. This makes no harm in the context of the paper; in any case, a failure value for goals can be added to the language together with the failure propagation rules.

4   Relational Conversion

Before we describe the relational conversion itself, we formulate some limitations for the source programs. Functional programs tend to operate with higher-order values, while miniKanren is limited by a first-order unification. Therefore, it would be unreasonable to expect, that arbitrary functional program can be converted into a relational form (at least using reasonably simple transformations).

We introduce the set of ground types $\mathcal{G}$:

$$\mathcal{G} = \alpha \mid T^k(g_1, \ldots, g_k)$$

Informally, a value of a ground type cannot contain closures. Then we formulate the following limitations for the programs to be converted into a relational form:

- all constructor parameter types must be type variables;
- constructors and polymorphic equality can only be applied to the values of ground types;
- all <u>match</u>-expressions must be of ground types.

The first condition means, that all algebraic datatypes (which we consider as defined implicitly, see Sect. 3.1) have to be fully-polymorphic. The first two limitations then allow us to specify the polymorphism restriction for relational programs, which we mentioned informally in Sect. 2: all type variables are bounded to range only over ground types (this condition, of course, is sufficient, but not necessary).

The third limitation is not essential and introduced only to simplify the presentation. If a <u>match</u>-expression does not have a ground type, it can always be transformed to have one by applying η-expansion:

$$\underline{\text{match}} \ e \ \underline{\text{with}} \ \{p_i \rightarrow e_i\} \ \rightsquigarrow \ \lambda \bar{x}.\underline{\text{match}} \ e \ \underline{\text{with}} \ \{p_i \rightarrow e_i \, \bar{x}\}$$

where $\bar{x}$ is a vector of new variables, different from those in e, e_i, and p_i. In fact, our implementation, described in Sect. 5, performs this expansion as long as a non-ground type <u>match</u>-expression is encountered. This is the single case when we actually inspect types and perform η-expansion.

The general idea behind the conversion can be illustrated on a type level: an expression of type t in the source language is transformed into the expression of type $[\![t]\!]^t$ in relational extension, where the transformation $[\![\bullet]\!]^t$ is defined as follows:

$$[\![g]\!]^t = g \to \mathfrak{G}$$
$$[\![t_1 \to t_2]\!]^t = [\![t_1]\!]^t \to [\![t_2]\!]^t$$

In other words, an expression of a ground type is converted into a goal-returning function. The informal semantics of this function is to make its argument respect a certain contract. As the argument can have some free variable occurrences, the goal tries to substitute these variables with some values in order to respect the contract this goal represents. For example, a constant `Nil` is converted into a function $\lambda q \ . \ q \equiv {\uparrow}\texttt{Nil}$.

The conversion itself is described in terms of transformation $[\![\bullet]\!]^c$, see Fig. 9. The first five rules simply propagate the conversion through the expression; the last three actually do the work. These rules themselves may look complicated, but the idea is rather simple.

In the case of constructor we know, that all expressions e_i have ground types. Thus, their relational images are goal-returning functions. We create a set of fresh variables (one for each expression) and pass them as arguments to these functions to associate them with the values of the expressions. The result of conversion for the constructor application itself has to be a goal-returning function as well. We surround expression constructed so far with abstraction and unify its argument q with the constructor, applied to corresponding logical variables. We also apply logical constructor $\uparrow$ to respect the typing rule for unification.

The rule for pattern-matching conversion operates similarly. First, the scrutinee must have a ground type (since it is matched against constructors). We create a fresh variable q_e and associate it with the value of the scrutinee exactly as in the previous case. Then, for each branch we create a number of fresh variables (one for each variable in the pattern for the branch) and express pattern-matching in terms of unification, using these variables and corresponding constructor. Finally, the body e_i of the branch is an expression with free variables, corresponding to those in the pattern. We, therefore, convert e_i and surround the result with lambdas, closing all these variables. To pass the bindings q_j^i for pattern variables to the body, we apply this function to goal-returning functions ($\equiv q_j^i$). This, again, gives us a goal-returning function, which we apply to the topmost result variable q.

The last rule follows the same pattern: both arguments of polymorphic equality are transformed into goal-returning functions, and we know, that the arguments of these functions are of some ground type. We apply these functions to fresh variables and perform case analysis. Note, this is the only case when we actually use disequality constraints (Fig. 9).

An interesting property of relational conversion is that it does not change terms, which do not use constructors, equality, and pattern-matching. Thus, a lot of useful higher-order functions—application, composition, fixed point, etc.—are already relational and can be used in relational specifications.

Another observation is that our transformation is compositional (a relational image of application is an application of relational images). This means, that

$$[\![x]\!]^c = x$$
$$[\![\lambda x.e]\!]^c = \lambda x.[\![e]\!]^c$$
$$[\![f\ e]\!]^c = [\![f]\!]^c\ [\![e]\!]^c$$
$$[\![\underline{let}\ x = e_1\ \underline{in}\ e_2]\!]^c = \underline{let}\ x = [\![e_1]\!]^c\ \underline{in}\ [\![e_2]\!]^c$$
$$[\![\underline{let}\ \underline{rec}\ f = \lambda x.e_1\ \underline{in}\ e_2]\!]^c = \underline{let}\ \underline{rec}\ f = [\![\lambda x.e_1]\!]^c\ \underline{in}\ [\![e_2]\!]^c$$

$$[\![C^k(e_1,\ldots,e_k)]\!]^c = \lambda\ q.\underline{fresh}\ (q_1 \ldots q_k)$$
$$([\![e_1]\!]^c\ q_1)\ \wedge$$
$$\ldots$$
$$([\![e_k]\!]^c\ q_k)\ \wedge$$
$$(q \equiv \uparrow (C^n(q_1,\ldots,q_k)))$$

$$[\![\underline{match}\ e\ \underline{with}\ \{C_i^{n_i}(x_1^i,\ldots,x_{n_i}^i) \to e_i\}]\!]^c = \lambda\ q.\underline{fresh}\ (q_e)$$
$$([\![e]\!]^c\ q_e)\ \wedge$$
$$\bigvee_i\ ((\underline{fresh}\ (q_1^i \ldots q_{n_i}^i)$$
$$(q_e \equiv \uparrow C_i^{n_i}(q_1^i,\ldots,q_{n_i}^i))\ \wedge$$
$$(\lambda\ x_1^i \ldots x_{n_i}^i.[\![e_i]\!]^c)\ (\equiv q_1^i)\ \ldots\ (\equiv q_{n_i}^i)\ q$$
$$)$$
$$)$$

$$[\![e_1 = e_2]\!]^c = \lambda\ q.\underline{fresh}\ (q_1\ q_2)$$
$$[\![e_1]\!]^c\ q_1\ \wedge$$
$$[\![e_2]\!]^c\ q_2\ \wedge$$
$$((q_1 \equiv q_2\ \wedge q \equiv \uparrow\underline{true})\ \vee$$
$$(q_1 \not\equiv q_2\ \wedge q \equiv \uparrow\underline{false})$$
$$)$$

Fig. 9. Relational conversion

relational conversion is compatible with separate compilation—multiple source files can be converted independently without losing the possibility to work properly when combined.

Then, it is interesting, that the result of relational conversion runs in a forward direction deterministically. Thus, relational conversion imposes only a constant-time slowdown in a forward direction.

Finally, we formulate the following properties for relational conversion:

- Static correctness: if an expression e has a type t in the source language, then $[\![e]\!]^c$ has a type $[\![t]\!]^t$ in relational extension. In other words, relational conversion transforms properly typed programs into properly typed. Proof is by structural induction (and trivial).
- Partial semantic correctness: if an expression e has a ground type t and $e \leadsto^f v$ for some value v, then $\underline{fresh}(x)([\![e]\!]^c\ x) \leadsto^r (\theta,\varnothing)$, and $\theta(\mathfrak{s}) = v$, where $\mathfrak{s}$ is a semantic variable, associated with x on the first step of the relational evaluation.

In order to prove the complete correctness, we need some means to interpret the results of relational derivation with free variables in functional case. This is a subject of future research.

5   Implementation and Application

We implemented relational conversion for the subset of OCaml language, using the infrastructure of the original compiler. In its current form, the converter takes the whole file and converts every definition into relational form, but in future, we consider to implement a more flexible approach, when only some definitions are converted, being attributed for this purpose in some way. Our converter rewrites the original abstract syntax tree, annotated with the types, inferred by the compiler, into relational form, using the set of combinators from OCanren. Note, the semantics of OCaml is different from the semantics of source language we presented in Sect. 3.1: in OCaml, the order of reductions in application and binary operators is unspecified (unlike left-to-right in our case), pattern-matching in OCaml is performed in a top-down manner (and, thus, there can be more than one pattern matching the scrutinee), etc. We, therefore, trust an end user to apply relational conversion only to programs, for which these differences play no role.

Our preliminary evaluation discovered two problems. First, the converter used to generate a lot of abstractions, many of which could be applied immediately. We additionally implemented an optimization pass, which performs administrative reductions where possible. This optimization greatly improves the quality of converted programs in terms of both readability and performance. Next, in our initial implementation, too many values were functionalized and, as a result, massively recalculated with essential performance degradation. We improved the implementation by identifying the important specific case and handling it with a little different transformation.

As the first example of the conversion we consider the implementation of concatenation function for lists (see Fig. 10a). In Sect. 2, we already saw the canonical version of relational concatenation. The result of relational conversion, however, is slightly different (see Fig. 10b). The main difference comes from the

```
val append : α list →            val appendᵒ : ((α llist)ᵒ → Ⓖ) →
               α list →                         ((α llist)ᵒ → Ⓖ) →
               α list                           (α llist)ᵒ → Ⓖ
let rec append = λ a.λ b.        let rec appendᵒ a b q1 =
   match a with                     fresh (q2)
   | Nil          → b                  (a q2) ∧
   | Cons (h, t) →                     (((q2 ≡ ↑Nil) ∧ (b q1)) ∨
        Cons (h, append t b)           (fresh (q3 q4)
                                          (q2 ≡ ↑(Cons (q3, q4))) ∧
                                          (fresh (q6 q7)
                                             (q6 ≡ q3) ∧
                                             (q1 ≡ ↑(Cons (q6, q7))) ∧
                                             (appendᵒ (≡ q4) b q7))))
            (a)                                      (b)
```

Fig. 10. An example of relational conversion

functionalization of primitive values: while conventional append^o operates on logical lists, the converted variant uses a goal-returning functions. Thus, the conventional append^o for arguments x, y and q can be expressed using the converted one as append^o ($\equiv$x) ($\equiv$y) q.

In the next subsections, we consider more elaborated and interesting examples. From now on, we refrain from presenting the complete source and converted code and consider only the signatures and some interesting queries.

5.1   Higher-Order Lambda Interpreter

As we mentioned in Sect. 1, one of the important application domains for miniKanren is the implementation of relational interpreters [5,6,8]. Writing relational interpreter, as a rule, amounts to a careful rewriting of functional implementation in miniKanren. In this regard, obtaining a relational interpreter automatically from a functional specification looks a natural idea.

In our case, we generalize this idea a little bit: we build a relational interpreter for a family of languages—essentially, the lambda calculus with various reduction orders. The construction of this interpreter was inspired by Felleisen-style semantic description [16]. Our interpreter takes as its first argument a function, which decomposes a term, passed as a second argument, into a redex and a context (if possible). After the decomposition, the interpreter performs beta-reduction on the redex and reconstructs the term by plugging the result back into the context. These steps are repeated until the decomposition is no longer possible (or infinitely). This approach brings us a few benefits: first, various reduction orders can be expressed by changing only the decomposition function, and next, we demonstrate the applicability of our technique for a higher-order case.

The signatures of relevant functions are

```
val eval : (term  →  split)  →  term  →  term
val call_by_name  : term  →  split
val call_by_value : term  →  split
val normal_order  : term  →  split
```

where term and split are the types of the terms (in de Bruijn form) and context-term pairs respectively; eval is a higher-order interpreter, all other functions define corresponding reduction orders. Relational counterparts for these definitions, provided by the conversion, are shown below:

```
val eval°  : ((term°  → ℧)  → split°  → ℧)  → (term°  → ℧)  →
             term°  → ℧
val call_by_name°  : (term°  → ℧)  → split°  → ℧
val call_by_value° : (term°  → ℧)  → split°  → ℧
val normal_order°  : (term°  → ℧)  → split°  → ℧
```

Note, due to the compositionality of the conversion, the type of functions, representing reduction orders, still corresponds to the type of the first argument of the interpreter.

The interpreter, constructed by our tool, can be run in a forward direction (for readability purposes, we use here a symbolic quoted representation of the terms instead of concrete datatype constructor-based):

```
eval° normal_order° (≡ '(λ 0) 1') q ⤳ [q ↦ '1']
eval° call_by_name° (≡ '0 ((λ 0) 1)') q ⤳ [q ↦ '0 ((λ 0) 1)']
eval° call_by_value° (≡ '0 ((λ 0) 1)') q ⤳ [q ↦ '0 1']
```

As it is expected from relational interpreter, it equally can be run in the opposite direction, returning for a term a (potentially infinite) stream of terms, reducing to it:

```
eval° normal_order° (≡ q) ('λ 0') ⤳ [
    q ↦ 'λ 0';
    q ↦ '(λ 0) (λ 0)';
    q ↦ 'λ ((λ 1) 0 )';
    q ↦ '(λ 0) ((λ 0) (λ 0))'; ...]
eval° call_by_name° (≡ q) ('λ 0') ⤳ [
    q ↦ 'λ 0';
    q ↦ '(λ 0) (λ 0)';
    q ↦ '(λ 0) ((λ 0) (λ 0))';
    q ↦ '(λ λ 0) 0'; ...]
```

This interpreter can be extended to the subset of Scheme, with which the quines/twines/thrines benchmarks [8] can be reproduced.

5.2 Hindley-Milner Type Inference

Our next example is the type inference for Hindley-Milner type system [15]. Interestingly enough, that while typing rules for STLC can be directly expressed in relational terms, providing the solutions for type inference, type checking, and type inhabitation problems at the same time, for not so different Hindley-Milner system with let-polymorphism, the problem becomes much harder. The most robust existing relational solution requires the extension of miniKanren with nominal constructs [7], while the correctness of other implementations in conventional miniKanren is still a matter of discussion [4].

On the other hand, in terms of functional programming, this task is rather a textbook exercise. We implemented a simple version of syntax-directed type inference and converted it into the relational form; the signatures for the original and converted implementations are shown below:

```
val type_inference  : term → typ
val type_inference° : (term° → ᵒ) → typ° → ᵒ
```

For this example, we use a conventional representation of terms with named variables. In a forward direction, our relational implementation works, as expected, as a type inferencer—given a term it infers its type:

```
type_inference° (≡ 'λx → x') q ⤳ [q ↦ 'a → a']
```

In a reverse direction, relational type inferencer is capable of finding the inhabitants of a specified type:

```
type_inference° (≡ q) 'a' ⤳ ⊥
type_inference° (≡ q) 'a → a' ⤳ [
    q ↦ 'λ 0 → 0 ';
    q ↦ 'λ 0 → (λ 1 → 1 ) 0 ';
    q ↦ 'λ 0 → let 1 = 2 in 0 ' ( 0 ≢ 1 );
    q ↦ '(λ 0 → 0 ) (λ 1 → 1 )'; ...]
```

Note, the first query diverges, providing no results (which is rather expected since the type is un-inhabited). This is a long-time known phenomenon of miniKanren—the search can diverge, when no answers exist; relational specifications, which always stop in this case, are called *refutationally complete* [5]. Given example demonstrates, that our derived relational specification is not refutationally complete, which is not a rarity in the relational world; making it refutationally complete is a separate task.

It may appear at first glance, that using relational Hindley-Milner inferencer for solving inhabitance problem is superfluous, since the inhabitance for Hindley-Milner is equivalent to inhabitance for STLC. However, with relational inferencer we may solve some problems, which are distinct from both pure inference and pure inhabitance:

```
type_inference° (≡ 'let f = □ in f (λ x → f x)') 'a → a' ⤳
    [□ ↦ 'λ 0 → 0 '; ...]
```

In this query, we supplied an *incomplete* term with a hole (□) and some type, and as a result, we've got a term to plug into the hole in order for the complete term to have that type. Note, the term we've got as a result cannot be typed in STLC, since the variable f is applied there twice with different types of arguments.

A final observation: we do not claim to completely solve the problem of relational implementation of Hindley-Milner type system. Even though our converted relational implementation behaves as expected, it still not ideal—indeed, in functional implementation we had to implement unification on types, which does not make use of built-in unification in miniKanren and, to some extent, doubles the work. We, therefore, do not consider this approach as an ideal solution.

5.3 miniKanren with Disequality Constraints

Our final example is an implementation of miniKanren in miniKanren. Although there already exist a few similar implementations, written directly in miniKanren, our version is different, since it supports disequality constraints. We consider this as an important distinction—first, the presence of disequality constraints makes the language much more expressible, and next, implementing disequality constraints directly in miniKanren is a very tedious and error-prone task. On the other hand, providing relationally converted version amounts only to repeating a well-known and rather compact original implementation [1].

The signatures for functional and relational miniKanren implementations are as follows:

```
val mk  : goal  → substitution list
val mkᵒ : (goalᵒ → Ⓖ) → (substitution llist)ᵒ → Ⓖ
```

Here `goal` stands for the type, representing the goals, `substitution`—for the type of substitutions. Again, our relational miniKanren interpreter works in both directions. As a more interesting query, we consider the following:

$$mk^o$$

$$(\equiv$$

```
'let rec add a b c =
    ((a ≡ Z) ∧ (b ≡ c)) ∨
    (fresh (a₀ c₀) (a ≡ S a₀) ∧ □ ∧ (add a₀ b c₀))
  in fresh (x y z) (add x y z)') ([[x='1'; y='1'; z='2']])  ⇝
[□ ↦ 'c ≡ S c₀'; ...]
```

Here we specified an incomplete relational program (specifically, a relational addition of numbers in Peano form). The hole ($\square$) replaces one of the branches, and expected substitution describes the results of addition. Our relational interpreter, converted from functional implementation, turned out to be capable of finding the correct subgoal—" $c \equiv S\ c_0$ "—to be placed into the hole.

6   Conclusion

We presented an approach for converting typed functional programs into relations. Relational conversion in many cases allows us to avoid tedious recoding of functional specifications into relational form and to concentrate on writing relational specifications only when their reconstruction from functions is impossible or undesirable. Our implementation works for the subset of OCaml; we evaluated it for a number of interesting examples and acquired some new relational solutions.

There is a number of directions for future research. First, a performance evaluation is desirable—at present time we do not know, what slowdown factor is. Another problem is a development of an approach to prove complete correctness (or refute this claim).

References

1. Alvis, C.E., Willcock, J.J., Carter, K.M., Byrd, W.E., Friedman, D.P.: cKanren: miniKanren with constraints. In: Proceedings of the 2011 Annual Workshop on Scheme and Functional Programming, October 2011
2. Baader, F., Snyder, W.: Unification theory. In: Handbook of Automated Reasoning. Elsevier Science Publishers B.V., Amsterdam (2001)

3. Barendregt, H.P.: Lambda calculi with types. In: Handbook of Logic in Computer Science, vol. 2, pp. 117–309. Oxford University Press Inc., New York (1992)
4. Byrd, W.E.: Private communication
5. Byrd, W.E.: Relational programming in miniKanren: techniques, applications, and implementations. Ph.D. thesis, Indiana University, September 2009
6. Byrd, W.E., Ballantyne, M., Rosenblatt, G., Might, M.: A unified approach to solving seven programming problems (functional pearl). Proc. ACM Program. Lang. 1(ICFP), 8:1–8:26 (2017)
7. Byrd, W.E., Friedman, D.P.: αKanren: a fresh name in nominal logic programming. In: Proceedings of the 2007 Annual Workshop on Scheme and Functional Programming, pp. 79–90 (2007)
8. Byrd, W.E., Holk, E., Friedman, D.P.: miniKanren, live and untagged: quine generation via relational interpreters (programming pearl). In: Proceedings of the 2012 Annual Workshop on Scheme and Functional Programming, Scheme 2012, pp. 8–29. ACM, New York (2012)
9. Cardelli, L., Wegner, P.: On understanding types, data abstraction, and polymorphism. ACM Comput. Surv. 17(4), 471–523 (1985)
10. Friedman, D.P., Byrd, W.E., Kiselyov, O.: The Reasoned Schemer. The MIT Press, Cambridge (2005)
11. Hemann, J., Friedman, D.P.: μKanren: a minimal functional core for relational programming. In: Proceedings of the 2013 Annual Workshop on Scheme and Functional Programming (2013)
12. Hemann, J., Friedman, D.P., Byrd, W.E., Might, M.: A small embedding of logic programming with a simple complete search. SIGPLAN Not. 52(2), 96–107 (2016)
13. Kosarev, D., Boulytchev, D.: Typed embedding of a relational language in OCaml. In: ACM SIGPLAN Workshop on ML (2016)
14. Lassez, J.-L., Maher, M.J., Marriott, K.: Unification revisited. In: Foundations of Deductive Databases and Logic Programming, pp. 587–625. Morgan Kaufmann Publishers Inc., San Francisco (1988)
15. Pierce, B.C.: Types and Programming Languages, 1st edn. The MIT Press, Cambridge (2002)
16. Wright, A., Felleisen, M.: A syntactic approach to type soundness. Inf. Comput. 115(1), 38–94 (1994)

QuickChecking Patricia Trees

Jan Midtgaard[✉]

The Maersk Mc-Kinney Moller Institute, University of Southern Denmark,
Campusvej 55, 5230 Odense M, Denmark
mail@janmidtgaard.dk

Abstract. Patricia trees are a space-efficient, purely functional data
structure, useful for efficiently implementing both integer sets and dictionaries with integer keys. In this paper we illustrate how to build a
QuickCheck model of the data structure for the purpose of testing a
mature OCaml library implementing it. In doing so, we encounter a subtle bug, initially inherited from a paper by Okasaki and Gill, and since
then flying under the radar for almost two decades.

1 Introduction

Since data structures are at the heart of many applications it is important to
ensure their correctness. This becomes even more important as software modules
are often reused thanks to the growing popularity of open source software and
code-sharing platforms such as GitHub.

In this paper we illustrate how one can build a straightforward QuickCheck
model for testing Patricia trees, a commonly used functional data structure. In
doing so, we encounter a subtle bug in a common Patricia tree library, inherited from a published paper (Okasaki and Gill 1998). Our paper thereby serves
multiple purposes:

- as a tutorial example of building a QuickCheck model to unveil the bug,
- to document this error, and
- to illustrate the significance of generators for QuickChecking.

2 Background

We first recall the relevant background material on Patricia trees and
QuickCheck.

2.1 Patricia Trees

A *Patricia tree* is a data structure for representing integer sets (and dictionaries)
compactly and *functionally*. Historically Patricia trees were introduced 50 years
ago by Morrison (1968). Thirty years later they were recast as a functional data
structure and popularized by Okasaki and Gill (1998). The data structure works

© Springer International Publishing AG, part of Springer Nature 2018
M. Wang and S. Owens (Eds.): TFP 2017, LNCS 10788, pp. 59–78, 2018.
https://doi.org/10.1007/978-3-319-89719-6_4

by inspecting and traversing the underlying representation of a set's numbers bit by bit (alphanumerically). Below we explain the little endian version that traverses the bits from the least to the most significant bit.

Elements in a Patricia tree are ordered similarly to a standard binary search tree. Specifically the order of elements is determined by a *branching bit* in all internal nodes: elements with a 0 in the branching bit belong in the internal node's left sub-tree, whereas elements with a 1 in the branching bit belong in the internal node's right sub-tree. For example, the branching bit of the root node in the Patricia tree in Fig. 1 is the least significant bit (the *parity* bit, 0001, when we limit the presentation to only four bits). Therefore the even element 8 with bit representation (1000) belong to the left sub-tree, whereas the odd elements 5 (0101) and 13 (1101) belong to the right sub-tree. Similarly the branching bit of the root's right child is the fourth bit (1000) and lets us distinguish its two children (0101 and 1101).

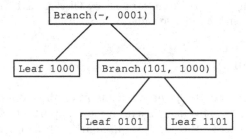

Fig. 1. The Patricia tree corresponding to the set $\{5, 8, 13\}$

To avoid needless branches the internal nodes of a Patricia tree also carry a shared *prefix* representing the string of bits that all elements in a given sub-tree have in common. For example, the elements 5 (0101) and 13 (1101) in Fig. 1 share the common prefix 101 but differ in the fourth bit (1000).

The ptrees library is a mature OCaml implementation of Patricia trees. For example, the Sawja library (Hubert et al. 2011) internally uses ptrees for efficient functional data structures, and Sawja is again used as the Java front-end in Facebook's static analyzer Infer (Calcagno and Distefano 2011). Like other data structures, such as red-black trees, we can use the Patricia tree structure to create both integer sets (by storing at each leaf only set-membership information) and to create dictionaries with integer keys (by storing at each leaf the entry associated with the given integer key). In ptrees this is realized by two sub-modules: One sub-module Ptset of ptrees implements integer sets whereas another sub-module Ptmap of ptrees represents dictionaries with integer keys.[1] In the following we will focus on the set implementation Ptset.[2]

---

[1] The most recent version has simply split ptrees into separate packages Ptset and Ptmap, both of which are available through OCaml's package manager OPAM.

[2] The module Ptset also contains a sub-module implementing a big-endian version following the description of Okasaki and Gill (1998).

Following Okasaki and Gill (1998), `Ptset` represents Patricia trees as an algebraic data type with three constructors:

```
type t =
  | Empty
  | Leaf of int
  | Branch of int * int * t * t
```

The first constructor `Empty` represents the empty set, the second constructor `Leaf` represents a singleton set, and the third constructor `Branch` splices together two sub-trees based on a shared prefix and a branching bit as explained above.

As an example operation, consider mem : `int -> t -> bool`, a membership predicate. The `mem` predicate can be implemented as a recursive function that pattern matches on the node type:

```
let zero_bit k bb = (k land bb) == 0
let rec mem k = function
  | Empty  -> false
  | Leaf j -> k == j
  | Branch (_, bb, l, r) ->
      mem k (if zero_bit k bb then l else r)
```

For empty trees and leaves mem's code is straightforward: empty sets contain no members and a singleton set {j} contains only j. For internal nodes we test whether the branching bit bb is zero (after extracting it by a suitable logical *and'ing*), and continue the search recursively in the left (or right) sub-tree.

One interesting fact about Patricia trees is that they have a unique representation, meaning that identical sets will have identical structure. For now we will not concern ourselves with how Patricia trees are implemented under the hood but rather take a black-box view of the `Ptset` module for testing purposes. To this end we limit ourselves to the following subset of operations to keep things manageable:

```
val empty     : Ptset.t
val singleton : int -> Ptset.t
val mem       : int -> Ptset.t -> bool
val add       : int -> Ptset.t -> Ptset.t
val remove    : int -> Ptset.t -> Ptset.t
val union     : Ptset.t -> Ptset.t -> Ptset.t
val inter     : Ptset.t -> Ptset.t -> Ptset.t
```

All of these should be self-explanatory as operations over integer sets. The `add` operation for example expects an integer and a Patricia tree as arguments and returns a new Patricia tree representing the resulting, bigger set.

2.2   QuickCheck

QuickCheck (Claessen and Hughes 2000) is also known as *(randomized) property-based testing*. As such, it builds on the idea of expressing a family of tests by a *property* (quantified over some input) and a *generator* of input. For the rest of this paper we will use OCaml's QCheck library.[3] As an example, consider McCarthy's 91 function:

```
let rec mc x =
  if x > 100 then x - 10 else mc (mc (x + 11))
```

This function is renown for being observably equivalent to the following simpler specification:

$$mc(n) = \begin{cases} 91 & n \le 101 \\ n - 10 & n > 101 \end{cases}$$

(if we allow ourselves to ignore stack overflows due to the heavy use of recursion).

To test this property, we supply Test.make with the equivalence property and an input generator small_signed_int (a builtin generator of small signed integers from the QCheck library) to form a QuickCheck test:

```
let mc91_spec =
  Test.make ~name:"McCarthy_91_corr._spec" ~count:1000
    small_signed_int
    (fun n -> if n <= 101
              then mc n = 91
              else mc n = n - 10)
```

where we additionally specify the name of the tested property and the number of desired test runs (1000) as optional parameters ~name and ~count. We can subsequently run this QuickCheck test:

```
QCheck_runner.run_tests ~verbose:true [mc91_spec]
```

and confirm the specification over the generated, small integer inputs:

```
law McCarthy 91 corr. spec: 1000 relevant cases (1000 total)
success (ran 1 tests)
```

Suppose we instead phrase a test of the incorrect property that McCarthy's 91 function is equivalent to the constant function always returning 91:

```
let mc91_const =
  Test.make ~name:"McCarthy_91_constant" ~count:1000
    small_signed_int (fun n -> mc n = 91)
```

and run it, QCheck will immediately inform us of this failed property and print a minimal (*shrunk*) input for which it fails:

```
law McCarthy 91 constant: 3 relevant cases (3 total)
  test `McCarthy 91 constant`
  failed on ≥ 1 cases:
  102 (after 30 shrink steps)
```

In this case it took the QCheck library 30 simplification steps to cut a failing input down to this minimal one, 102. Such shrinking is important in trying to understand the (often large) machine generated counterexamples on which a property fails. For example, if we disable the default, builtin shrinking over integers we may get a larger counterexample:

---

[3] Available at https://github.com/c-cube/qcheck/.

```
law McCarthy 91 constant: 8 relevant cases (8 total)
 test 'McCarthy 91 constant' failed on ≥ 1 cases: 4921
```

From the input 4921 it may be less clear what the underlying problem is.

In the Erlang community it is common to combine the randomized property-based testing approach with that of *model-based testing* (Hughes 2010; Arts and Castro 2011). Concretely, this involves expressing an abstract model of the system (or module) under test and to test each of the available operations '*op*' for the property

the model and the implementation of 'op' agree

akin to how we have tested agreement between McCarthy's 91 function and its specification. For this reason the commercial QuickCheck implementation offered by Quviq comes with a domain-specific language (DSL) for compactly expressing

- models,
- generators of arbitrary sequences of operations, and
- the above agreement property.

However we do not need such a DSL to express a model (Claessen and Hughes 2002; Arts et al. 2008). In the next section we will build an example model.

3   Building a Model

Following practice within the QuickCheck community (Claessen and Hughes 2002; Hughes 2010), we build a *model* of Patricia trees that distills their functionality to its core. Unlike the established Erlang tradition (Hughes 2010; Arts and Castro 2011) we will explicitly express a model, a symbolic representation of operation sequences, a generator of arbitrary sequences of operations, and the agreement property. The following subsections are concerned with each of these.

3.1   A Model

A *model* serves as an executable specification of the intended meaning of a piece of software, similarly to how a *definitional interpreter* (Reynolds 1972) specifies the intended meaning (the semantics) of a programming language. When Patricia trees are used to implement integer sets, we can easily model them using a list. For example, an empty set can be modeled with an empty list, a singleton set can be modeled with a singleton list, and the membership predicate can be delegated to List.mem from the standard library (assuming it has been thoroughly tested):

```
let empty_m = []
let singleton_m i = [i]
let mem_m i s = List.mem i s
```

where we suffix the operations with _m to underline that these operations belong to our model.

The distinguishing feature of sets, namely uniqueness of elements, surfaces when building a model for the remaining operations. For these we choose to maintain a sorted list representation. Based on this choice we can now implement a model straightforwardly. For example:

```
let add_m i s =
  if List.mem i s then s else List.sort compare (i::s)
```

where we rely on `List.sort : ('a -> 'a -> int) -> 'a list -> 'a list` which expects a comparison function as its first argument.

The model for set union structurally recurses over its two argument lists, always puts the least element first, and thereby maintains the sorted invariant:

```
let rec union_m s s' = match s,s' with
  | [], _ -> s'
  | _, [] -> s
  | i::is,j::js -> if i<j then i::(union_m is s') else
                     if i>j then j::(union_m s js) else
                       i::(union_m is js)
```

The remaining models for `remove` and `inter` are straightforward and therefore omitted here.

In our situation of testing a *functional* data structure, the model may simply be regarded as an obviously correct but inefficient implementation of the abstract data type of sets (Arts et al. 2008). The model-based QuickCheck approach was initially suggested (among others) for testing monadic code (Claessen and Hughes 2002) and has since been used successfully and repeatedly for locating defects in imperative code such as Google's LevelDB key-value data storage library[4] and the underlying AUTOSAR modules used in Volvo cars (Hughes 2016).

3.2 Symbolic Operations

We first formulate a data type for symbolically representing calls to the `Ptset` API:

```
type instr_tree =
  | Empty
  | Singleton of int
  | Add of int * instr_tree
  | Remove of int * instr_tree
  | Union of instr_tree * instr_tree
  | Inter of instr_tree * instr_tree
```

Each of these constructors correspond to one of the operations listed earlier. The `Add` constructor for example represents the `add : int -> Ptset.t -> Ptset.t` operation from the API. It expects an integer (the element to be added) and a sub-tree representing the set the element is to be added to.

The alert reader may have noticed that we did not include a symbolic `Mem` constructor. The reason for this omission is simple: since a Patricia tree is a

---

[4] http://www.quviq.com/google-leveldb/.

functional data structure, a query cannot affect it. For the purposes of representing and generating arbitrary Patricia trees a mem-query therefore has no effect. We will of course include a test for agreement between mem and mem_m in our forthcoming test suite to exercise the operation.

We can now write an interpreter for such instruction trees. Following the inductive definition the interpreter becomes a recursive function that interprets each symbolic operation as the corresponding Patricia tree operation:

```
(*  interpret : instr_tree -> Ptset.t  *)
let rec interpret t = match t with
 | Empty          -> Ptset.empty
 | Singleton n    -> Ptset.singleton n
 | Add (n,t)      -> Ptset.add n (interpret t)
 | Remove (n,t)   -> Ptset.remove n (interpret t)
 | Union (t,t') ->
   let s  = interpret t in
   let s' = interpret t' in
   Ptset.union s s'
 | Inter (t,t') ->
   let s  = interpret t in
   let s' = interpret t' in
   Ptset.inter s s'
```

For example, we interpret a Singleton i node as a call to Ptset.singleton i and we interpret a Union node by two recursive interpretations of the sub-trees and a Ptset.union of their results.

3.3   A Generator

In order to QuickCheck the above properties we need the ability to generate arbitrary trees of operations. Starting from the inside, the below expresses a recursive generator expressed using QCheck's Gen.fix combinator:

```
(*  tree_gen : int Gen.t -> instr_tree Gen.t  *)
let tree_gen int_gen =
  Gen.sized (Gen.fix (fun rgen n -> match n with
   | 0 -> Gen.oneof [Gen.return Empty;
                     Gen.map (fun i -> Singleton i) int_gen]
   | _ ->
     Gen.frequency
       [(1,Gen.return Empty);
        (1,Gen.map  (fun i -> Singleton i) int_gen);
        (2,Gen.map2 (fun i t -> Add (i,t)) int_gen (rgen (n-1)));
        (2,Gen.map2 (fun i t -> Remove (i,t)) int_gen (rgen (n-1)));
        (2,Gen.map2 (fun l r -> Union (l,r)) (rgen (n/2)) (rgen (n/2)));
        (2,Gen.map2 (fun l r -> Inter (l,r)) (rgen (n/2)) (rgen (n/2)))
       ]))
```

Each invocation accepts a *fuel* parameter n to delimit the number of recursive generator calls. When we run out of fuel (n = 0), we hit the first branch of the pattern match and generate either a symbolic empty set or a singleton set. If there is still fuel left we choose between generating a list of things: empty sets, singletons, adds, removes, unions, or intersections. Since the latter four involves generating sub-trees we invoke the generator recursively, this time with a decreased amount of fuel. By the design of QCheck's fixed-point generator Gen.fix the recursive generator is passed as a parameter (above named rgen). For flexibility we have parameterized the tree generator over the integer generator int_gen used in the singleton, add, and remove cases. We thereby avoid having to rewrite the tree generator to experiment with integer generation.

To increase the chance of generating adds, removes, unions, or intersections we assign them a higher weight (2), meaning that each of them will be chosen with probability $\frac{2}{1+1+2+2+2+2} = \frac{1}{5}$ whereas an empty set or a singleton is only generated with probability only $\frac{1}{10}$. Finally we wrap the size-bounded, recursive generator in a call to QCheck's Gen.sized combinator, which first generates an arbitrary (small) integer and subsequently passes it as the fuel parameter to the size-bounded generator.

With the tree generator in place we can generate arbitrary trees from the top level. For example:

```
# Gen.generate1 (tree_gen Gen.int);;
- : Qctest.instr_tree =
Union
 (Union
   (Union (Add (1247377935267464492, Singleton (-344203684848058197)),
          Remove (788172988455234350, Empty)),
    Add (3495994339175018836, Singleton (-3950939914241702626))),
  Add (1460909625285095467,
      Inter (Singleton 3576840527525220675,
             Union (Empty, Singleton (-534074627919219807)))))))
```

where we pass Gen.int as integer generator (a uniform generator of int).

Since OCaml does not supply a generic printer for use outside the top level, QCheck cannot print our trees in case it should find a counterexample. It is however straightforward to write (yet another) structural, recursive function to_string that serializes a symbolic instruction tree into a string. We can now express our generator with printing capability as follows:

```
(*  arb_tree : instr_tree arbitrary *)
let arb_tree = make ~print:to_string (tree_gen Gen.int)
```

where we make use of QCheck's make operation for combining the pure generator resulting from tree_gen with our pretty-printer to_string into a full generator (these are denoted by the parameterized type 'a arbitrary in QCheck).

3.4 Expressing Agreement

To express agreement between the implementation and our abstract model we need a final piece of the puzzle: the ability to relate one to the other. Following Claessen and Hughes (2002), we can do so with an abstraction function abstract : Ptset.t -> int list. We can simply implement abstract as an alias for the elements operation from the earlier versions of ptrees's set API. In the recent API versions however, elements has been removed. In this case we can easily implement it as a fold, followed by a subsequent sorting:

```
let abstract s =
  List.sort compare (Ptset.fold (fun i a -> i::a) s [])
```

At last we are in position to test! For example we can write a test that expresses agreement between the singleton operation over both Patricia trees and our model:

```
let singleton_test =
  Test.make ~name:"singleton_test" ~count:10000
    arb_int (fun n -> abstract (Ptset.singleton n) = singleton_m n)
```

This expresses that creating a singleton set as a Patricia tree and abstracting the result as an ordered list should agree with our model interpretation over lists.

Similarly we can express agreement for the union operation:

```
let union_test =
  Test.make ~name:"union_test" ~count:10000
    (pair arb_tree arb_tree)
    (fun (t,t') ->
      let s  = interpret t in
      let s' = interpret t' in
      abstract (Ptset.union s s') = union_m (abstract s) (abstract s'))
```

This expresses that the elements of two joined Patricia trees should give the same as taking the union of the elements for each tree.

3.5   Shrinking Trees

A sometimes neglected advantage of QuickCheck is *shrinking*: the ability to systematically cut down large machine-generated counterexamples to small ones that are easier for humans to understand. This mirrors the working routine of a software engineer: first recreate a run with an input exhibiting a bug, then systematically cut down the input (if possible) to a minimum in order to get to the heart of the error.

In QCheck shrinkers are implemented as iterators: a lazy stream of values. For example, Iter.empty creates the empty stream, Iter.return v creates the singleton stream containing only v, Iter.of_list vs creates a stream from a list vs, and Iter.append sequences two iterator streams (it is also available under the infix alias <+>).

We can now express our shrinker as follows:

```
(* tshrink : instr_tree -> instr_tree Iter.t  *)
let rec tshrink t = match t with
  | Empty -> Iter.empty
  | Singleton i ->
    (Iter.return Empty)
    <+> (Iter.map (fun i' -> Singleton i') (Shrink.int i))
```

```
  | Add (i,t) ->
    (Iter.of_list [Empty; t; Singleton i])
    <+> (Iter.map (fun t' -> Add (i,t')) (tshrink t))
    <+> (Iter.map (fun i' -> Add (i',t)) (Shrink.int i))
  | Remove (i,t) ->
    (Iter.of_list [Empty; t])
    <+> (Iter.map (fun t' -> Remove (i,t')) (tshrink t))
    <+> (Iter.map (fun i' -> Remove (i',t)) (Shrink.int i))
  | Union (t0,t1) ->
    (Iter.of_list [Empty;t0;t1])
    <+> (Iter.map (fun t0' -> Union (t0',t1)) (tshrink t0))
    <+> (Iter.map (fun t1' -> Union (t0,t1')) (tshrink t1))
  | Inter (t0,t1) ->
    (Iter.of_list [Empty;t0;t1])
    <+> (Iter.map (fun t0' -> Inter (t0',t1)) (tshrink t0))
    <+> (Iter.map (fun t1' -> Inter (t0,t1')) (tshrink t1))
```

This shrinker codifies a systematic reduction: (a) We cannot reduce empty trees further. (b) We attempt to first replace a singleton with an empty tree, and otherwise shrink the singleton element itself. (c) We attempt to first replace addition and removal nodes with an empty tree, by dropping the node and keeping only the sub-tree, by replacing an addition node with a singleton node, by shrinking the sub-tree recursively, or by reducing the added or removed element. (d) In both the remove, union, and intersection cases, we first attempt to replace them with an empty tree, we then attempt to keep only a sub-tree, and finally we attempt to reduce sub-trees recursively.

With tshrink for shrinking trees, we enhance our generator with this ability:

```
(*  arb_tree : instr_tree arbitrary *)
let arb_tree =
  make ~print:to_string ~shrink:tshrink (tree_gen arb_int.gen)
```

where arb_int is some integer generator.

3.6 Refining the Integer Generator

We have expressed all tests in terms of arb_int, an (unspecified) integer generator. If we run our tests with arb_int implemented as a uniform generator Gen.int everything appears to work as intended:

```
random seed: 33309109
law empty: 1 relevant cases (1 total)
law singleton test: 10000 relevant cases (10000 total)
law mem test: 10000 relevant cases (10000 total)
law add test: 10000 relevant cases (10000 total)
law remove test: 10000 relevant cases (10000 total)
law union test: 10000 relevant cases (10000 total)
law inter test: 10000 relevant cases (10000 total)
success (ran 7 tests)
```

Here we have tested the agreement property between the model and Ptset across the 7 operations, each on 10.000 arbitrary inputs, with the exception of empty which we only need to test once. Repeating this run (with different seeds for each run) does not change our perception. For example, if we repeat these 60.001 tests 10 times, totaling 600.010 tests the Patricia tree implementation still appears to function correctly.

The strategy of generating integers uniformly for our test cases may however be questioned. First, the chance of generating duplicate integer elements, e.g., for testing the remove or mem operations on a present element is diminishing over OCaml's 63-bit integers (on a 64-bit machine). By replacing the integer generator with small_signed_int we have a much bigger chance of generating duplicate elements as illustrated by the following two generator samples:

```
# Gen.generate ~n:10 int.gen;;
- : int list =
[-1639748044049575280; -759399516701955582; -3888521258132306650;
 2042601493422231077; 1455013020240427543; -2271053503848477623;
 -4460690534604894851; 3544156611970260363; 3465820468547989432;
 -2702741295924950030]
# Gen.generate ~n:10 small_signed_int.gen;;
- : int list = [-75; 65; 2390; 76; -1; 6; -9; 6; -546; -787]
```

Notice how the integer 6 occurs twice in the last sample. Repeating the above test run with small_signed_int as the integer generator however does not reveal anything new: the Patricia tree implementation passes another 600.010 generated tests.

A second concern about both the int generator and the small_signed_int generator is the small chance of generating a corner case such as min_int or max_int: Each of these is only emitted by the uniform int generator with a probability of one out of 2^{63} with OCaml's 63-bit integers and the small_signed_int generator will never emit them. Yet the past decades of software engineering tells us precisely to remember to test such corner cases! How can we do so?

One way to adjust the integer generator to include such corner cases is to compose multiple different generators. For example, we can choose to either generate a small_signed_int (which includes the corner case 0), generate an integer uniformly (as above), or generate one of the two extremal corner cases:

```
let arb_int = frequency [(5,small_signed_int);
                         (3,int);
                         (1, oneofl [min_int;max_int])]
```

Here we have weighted each of these choices, by generating a small_signed_int with chance $\frac{5}{9}$, by generating an integer uniformly with chance $\frac{3}{9} = \frac{1}{3}$, and by generating min_int or max_int with chance $\frac{1}{9}$. Overall with this alternative integer generator we still have *some* chance of generating *all* integers, but the resulting distribution is skewed towards smaller numbers and corner cases both with a reasonable chance of occurring repeatedly.

3.7   The Bug and Some Potential Fixes

If we try to run the test suite with the refined integer generator arb_int the framework quickly locates a problem:

```
random seed: 448813938
law empty: 1 relevant cases (1 total)
law singleton test: 10000 relevant cases (10000 total)
law mem test: 10000 relevant cases (10000 total)
law add test: 10000 relevant cases (10000 total)
law remove test: 10000 relevant cases (10000 total)
law union test: 3363 relevant cases (3363 total)
   test 'union test'
   failed on ≥ 1 cases:
   (Add (-4611686018427387904, Singleton 0),
    Add (-4611686018427387904, Singleton 1)) (after 9 shrink steps)

law inter test: 10000 relevant cases (10000 total)
failure (1 tests failed, ran 7 tests)
```

We identify the number -4611686018427387904 as min_int, the least representable integer in 64-bit OCaml. With this in mind, the counterexample illustrates that a set union of the sets {min_int, 0} and {min_int, 1} does not yield {min_int, 0, 1}! What does it yield then? If one calls abstract on the resulting data structure it actually yields

```
[-4611686018427387904; -4611686018427387904; 0; 1]
```

with a duplicate min_int entry!

    To understand the problem we must reopen the black box of Ptset's implementation. First, since min_int is represented in 2-complement representation as a string of 0's with only a 1 in the sign bit, the left sub-tree resulting from add min_int (singleton 0) has the shape displayed on the left in Fig. 2. Similarly the right sub-tree resulting from add min_int (singleton 1) has the shape displayed on the right in Fig. 2. Now, the union operator simply performs a call to the internal merge operation, which is a recursive procedure for merging two Patricia trees:

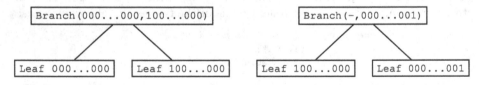

Fig. 2. The tree shapes resulting from add min_int (singleton 0) and add min_int (singleton 1)

```
1    let rec merge = function
2      | t1,t2 when t1==t2 -> t1
3      | Empty, t  -> t
4      | t, Empty  -> t
5      | Leaf k, t -> add k t
6      | t, Leaf k -> add k t
7      | (Branch (p,m,s0,s1) as s), (Branch (q,n,t0,t1) as t) ->
8        if m == n && match_prefix q p m then
9          (* The trees have the same prefix. Merge the subtrees. *)
10         Branch (p, m, merge (s0,t0), merge (s1,t1))
11       else if m < n && match_prefix q p m then
12         (* [q] contains [p]. Merge [t] with a subtree of [s]. *)
13         if zero_bit q m then
14           Branch (p, m, merge (s0,t), s1)
15         else
16           Branch (p, m, s0, merge (s1,t))
17       else if m > n && match_prefix p q n then
18         (* [p] contains [q]. Merge [s] with a subtree of [t]. *)
19         if zero_bit p n then
20           Branch (q, n, merge (s,t0), t1)
21         else
22           Branch (q, n, t0, merge (s,t1))
23       else
24         (* The prefixes disagree. *)
25         join (p, s, q, t)
```

The gist of the code is that it handles merging with empty sub-trees and leafs as separate cases (lines 3–6). In our situation above we hit the case of merging two branching nodes (line 7). This proceeds by a case analysis of the least significant branching bit: are the branching bits identical (and do the prefixes agree) (lines 8–10), is one branching bit less than the other (and do the prefixes agree) (lines 11–16 and 17–22), or is there some disagreement (lines 23–25)? In our case the branching bits are min_int and 1 and comparing them with a signed comparison (line 11) yields true contrasting the intention of taking the *least significant bit*. From here on it is downhill. The empty prefix (q, represented as all 0's) of the right tree also has a zero sign bit (line 13), thereby causing Leaf 000...000 to be merged recursively with the right tree (line 14). This boils down to invoking add (line 5) and results in a structure of the form:

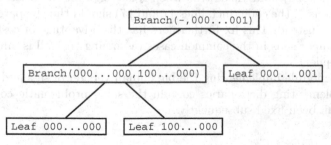

which is in turn placed as the left sub-tree in the overall result by line 14:

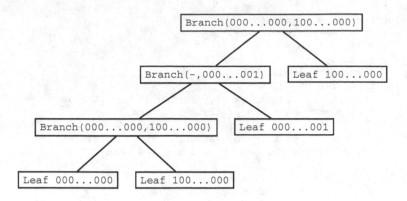

and thereby explains the duplicate entry of min_int in the result and the dis-agreement between the implementation and our model.

In retrospect, we now realize that our shrinker constructed a minimal coun-terexample: we need at least two branching nodes to hit line 7 and recreate the bug. In the current setting the error is also limited to a case with min_int occur-ring twice in order to be erroneously duplicated in the resulting list of elements. Subsequent runs with different seeds may of course produce different symbolic counterexamples all illustrating the same underlying issue.

One potential fix is to change the representation of the branching bit. After all we need only represent 63 different branching bit values on a 64-bit architecture which can be done with only 6 bits.[5] This fix is however a more invasive change throughout the module.

An elegant and less invasive patch was suggested by Jean-Christophe Filliâtre. The essence of the fix is to compare the two OCaml ints (a signed integer data type) albeit using an unsigned comparison. Since the only members we compare are branching bits on the binary form 0001, 0010, 0100, ..., we can do so as follows:

```
let unsigned_lt n m = n >= 0 && (m < 0 || n < m)
```

which boils down to n < m for all non-sign-bit cases, yields false when n is a sign-bit (as desired), and yields true when m is a sign-bit (as desired). All sign bit comparisons in the code (incl. lines 11 and 17) should thus be patched to call unsigned_lt instead. This fix furthermore has the advantage of costing only a few more comparisons in the common cases (assuming the call is inlined by the OCaml compiler).

The sub-module implementing the big endian version of sets and the Ptmap module implementing dictionaries contain the same problematic comparisons. They have all been fixed subsequently.

---

[5] OCaml's garbage collector reserves 1 *tag bit* in integers to distinguish them from heap-allocated data.

3.8   The Bug and the Research Paper

The identified bug is not only relevant to users of `ptrees`, but to the functional programming community at large. Compare the listed OCaml `merge` function to the following SML merge function from Okasaki and Gill (1998, Fig. 5):

```
1   fun merge c (s,t) =
2     let fun mrg (Empty, t) = t
3           | mrg (t, Empty) = t
4           | mrg (Lf (k,x), t) = insert c (k,x,t)
5           | mrg (t, Lf (k,x)) = (c o swap) (k,x,t)
6           | mrg (s as Br (p,m,s0,s1), t as Br (q,n,t0,t1)) =
7               if m=n andalso p=q then
8                   (* The trees have the same prefix. Merge the subtrees. *)
9                   Br (p,m,mrg (s0,t0),mrg (s1,t1))
10              else if m<n andalso matchPrefix (q,p,m) then
11                  (* q contains p. Merge t with a subtree of s. *)
12                  if zeroBit (q,m) then Br (p,m,mrg (s0,t),s1)
13                                  else Br (p,m,s0,mrg (s1,t))
14              else if m>n andalso matchPrefix (p,q,n) then
15                  (* p contains q. Merge s with a subtree of t. *)
16                  if zeroBit (p,n) then Br (q,n,mrg (s,t0),s1)
17                                  else Br (q,n,t0,mrg (s,t1))
18              else (* The prefixes disagree. *)
19                  join (p,s,q,t)
20    in mrg (s,t) end
```

where the parameter `c : 'a * 'a -> 'a` is a *combining function* for resolving key collisions (useful when Patricia trees are used to represent dictionaries in general).

The comments and the structure of this code are the same as in the OCaml version: lines 2–3 handle merging with empty trees, lines 4–5 handle merging with singletons, and lines 6–19 handle the merging of two internal nodes with a 4-branch case analysis like the OCaml version: are the branching bits identical (and do the prefixes agree) (lines 7–9), is one branching bit less than the other (and do the prefixes agree) (lines 10–13 and 14–17), or is there some disagreement (lines 18–19)?

The branching bit in the data type underlying the above operation is declared as SML's `int` type (also a signed integer data type):

```
datatype 'a Dict =
    Empty
  | Lf of int * 'a
  | Br of int * int * 'a Dict * 'a Dict
```

As Okasaki and Gill's `merge` function contains comparisons `m < n` and `m > n` written using the signed integer comparison of SML it thereby exhibits the same problematic behavior as the OCaml version.

Since the initial publication of our model, it has been reused by Simon Cruanes to QuickCheck the Patricia tree implementation in OCaml Containers, an extension of the OCaml standard library.[6] This merely required retargeting the

---

[6] https://github.com/c-cube/ocaml-containers.

interpretation of the symbolic operations. This alternative implementation had been developed independently and did not exhibit the bug.

4   Related Work

Over the past 17 years QuickCheck has evolved from a Haskell library (Claessen and Hughes 2000) to the present situation where ports have been made to many of the most popular programming languages.[7] In the process the approach has been extended to test imperative code (Claessen and Hughes 2002) and a commercial port for Erlang has been developed by the company Quviq. Quviq's commercial port includes a compact state-machine DSL for easily specifying and testing such code with *abstract models* (Hughes 2010) akin to the current paper. One notable difference between Quviq's state-machine DSL and the model in this paper is that

- the state-machine approach is sequence-centric: it can be used to generate API call sequences (at its core describing a *regular language*) and test agreement between a model and an implementation's output and behaviour, whereas
- the example model we have presented is tree-centric (describing a *context-free language*).

The API of Quviq's state-machine DSL has subsequently been mimicked in Erlang's open source QuickCheck libraries PropEr[8] and Triq[9]. Early on Gast for Clean (Koopman et al. 2003; Koopman and Plasmeijer 2005) supported compact and powerful state-based models, but for a number of years the situation for other languages was less promising. Only more recently has state-machine frameworks for other languages surfaced, such as ScalaCheck (Nilsson 2014) for Scala and Hedgehog[10] for Scala, F#, and Haskell.

We are certainly not the first to test a data structure using QuickCheck. Arts et al. (2008) present a general methodology to test abstract data types, exemplified by testing a 'decimal number type' (up to some rounding) against a model of floats. Their methodology is: (1) to define a model (and state equivalence), (2) to write as many equivalence properties as there are data type operations (and to work with a symbolic representation), (3) to write a generator, and (4) to define shrinking preferences (if needed). The methodology thereby spells out the model-based approach initially suggested by Claessen and Hughes (2002) and which we have also followed here. In a follow-up paper, Arts and Castro (2011) extend the methodology to test imperative data structures. This involves a combination of the Quviq state machine framework and boilerplate code generation of a test skeleton to keep the repetitive programming to a minimum.

---

[7] The Wikipedia page https://en.wikipedia.org/wiki/QuickCheck lists ports to 33 languages as of May 2017.

[8] http://proper.softlab.ntua.gr/.

[9] http://krestenkrab.github.io/triq/.

[10] https://github.com/hedgehogqa.

Since its introduction property-based testing has successfully been applied to test and locate errors in a broad class of software: formal semantics (Felleisen et al. 2009), election systems (Koopman and Plasmeijer 2011), optimizing compilers (Pałka et al. 2011; Midtgaard et al. 2017), type environments (St-Amour and Toronto 2013), dynamic analyzers (Hriţcu et al. 2013), type systems (Fetscher et al. 2015), static analyzers (Midtgaard and Møller 2015), and computational geometry (Sergey 2016). Common to many of these are that they are not model-based. For each particular domain, the involved operations are instead tested to satisfy domain-specific properties, e.g., non-interference (Hriţcu et al. 2013), lattice axioms (Midtgaard and Møller 2015), or geometric properties (Sergey 2016). Koopman et al. (2012) compare the bug-finding capabilities of the two forms of QuickCheck specifications: the traditional logical properties and input/output conformance in a state-machine framework. They conclude that both are powerful for detecting errors, but that the latter is slightly more effective.

Our refined integer generator arb_int is by no means the final word on integer generation. For some situations, e.g., our testing of McCarthy's 91 function, we would prefer to avoid generating duplicate numbers, as these represent redundant tests. In other situations (as we have argued) we would precisely want a generator to emit duplicates. An orthogonal aspect is size: the builtin generators of Quviq's commercial QuickCheck implementation is based on *generations*. The distribution of their integer generator int() thus initially generates smaller numbers but its output varies towards greater numbers as a property is repeatedly tested (generations goes by).[11] Testing and potentially catching errors over small inputs first will again reflect in time saved shrinking a needlessly big counterexample.

Recently there has been a trend towards letting a QuickCheck framework generalize the found counterexamples. SmartCheck (Pike 2014) is a QuickCheck extension that can perform such generalization with the goal of explaining the general erroneous behaviour to the user. MoreBugs (Hughes et al. 2016) is another QuickCheck extension performing such generalization with the goal of avoiding repeated rediscovery of the same bugs. In practice this becomes a concern if a tester does not want to pause the testing process until the first round of errors is fixed or adjust his model specification to reflect the code's buggy behaviour (Hughes 2016).

5   Conclusion and Perspectives

We have demonstrated how QuickCheck can locate a subtle bug in a published data structure paper after almost two decades—a bug which was also present in an influential library implementation.

For the purpose of bug-finding, the quality of a QuickCheck library's built-in generators is of utmost importance. Simple uniform generators are unlikely to exercise the corner cases that one would typically test by hand. As a consequence,

---

[11] http://quviq.com/documentation/eqc/eqc_gen.html.

a passing QuickCheck test suite based on such generators may give users a false sense of certainty in an implementation. Furthermore, for a QuickCheck library to be successful, the ability to efficiently shrink counterexamples is essential. Otherwise, the machine generated counterexamples simply get too big to be comprehensible for a human being. For both of these aspects, the commercial Quviq QuickCheck implementation has a clear advantage, with several years of effort in refining and engineering its generators and shrinkers.

The full source code of our developed tests is available for download at https://github.com/jmid/qc-ptrees.

Acknowledgments. We thank Jesper Louis Andersen for sharing his expertise with alternative integer generators, Jean-Christophe Filliâtre for his Patricia tree library implementation and for promptly providing an elegant fix, Simon Cruanes for suggesting improvements to the code, the TFP'17 participants for questions and comments, and the anonymous referees for a number of suggestions that helped improve the presentation of this paper.

References

Arts, T., Castro, L.M.: Model-based testing of data types with side effects. In: Rikitake, K., Stenman, E. (eds.) Proceedings of the 10th ACM SIGPLAN Workshop on Erlang, Tokyo, Japan, 23 September 2011, pp. 30–38 (2011)

Arts, T., Castro, L.M., Hughes, J.: Testing Erlang data types with Quviq QuickCheck. In: Teoh, S.T., Horváth, Z. (eds.) Proceedings of the 7th ACM SIGPLAN Workshop on Erlang, Victoria, BC, Canada, 27 September 2008, pp. 1–8 (2008)

Calcagno, C., Distefano, D.: Infer: an automatic program verifier for memory safety of C programs. In: Bobaru, M., Havelund, K., Holzmann, G.J., Joshi, R. (eds.) NFM 2011. LNCS, vol. 6617, pp. 459–465. Springer, Heidelberg (2011). https://doi.org/10.1007/978-3-642-20398-5_33

Claessen, K., Hughes, J.: QuickCheck: a lightweight tool for random testing of haskell programs. In: Wadler, P. (ed.) Proceedings of the Fifth ACM SIGPLAN International Conference on Functional Programming (ICFP 2000), Montréal, Canada, pp. 53–64 (2000)

Claessen, K., Hughes, J.: Testing monadic code with QuickCheck. SIGPLAN Not. **37**(12), 47–59 (2002)

Felleisen, M., Findler, R.B., Flatt, M.: Semantics Engineering with PLT Redex. The MIT Press, Cambridge (2009)

Fetscher, B., Claessen, K., Pałka, M., Hughes, J., Findler, R.B.: Making random judgments: automatically generating well-typed terms from the definition of a type-system. In: Vitek, J. (ed.) ESOP 2015. LNCS, vol. 9032, pp. 383–405. Springer, Heidelberg (2015). https://doi.org/10.1007/978-3-662-46669-8_16

Hriţcu, C., Hughes, J., Pierce, B.C., Spector-Zabusky, A., Vytiniotis, D., de Amorim, A.A., Lampropoulos, L.: Testing noninterference, quickly. In: Morrisett, G., Uustalu, T. (eds.) Proceedings of the 18th ACM SIGPLAN International Conference on Functional Programming (ICFP 2013), Boston, MA, pp. 455–468, September 2013

Hubert, L., Barré, N., Besson, F., Demange, D., Jensen, T., Monfort, V., Pichardie, D., Turpin, T.: Sawja: static analysis workshop for Java. In: Beckert, B., Marché, C. (eds.) FoVeOOS 2010. LNCS, vol. 6528, pp. 92–106. Springer, Heidelberg (2011). https://doi.org/10.1007/978-3-642-18070-5_7

Hughes, J.: Software testing with QuickCheck. In: Horváth, Z., Plasmeijer, R., Zsók, V. (eds.) CEFP 2009. LNCS, vol. 6299, pp. 183–223. Springer, Heidelberg (2010). https://doi.org/10.1007/978-3-642-17685-2_6

Hughes, J.: Experiences with QuickCheck: testing the hard stuff and staying sane. In: Lindley, S., McBride, C., Trinder, P., Sannella, D. (eds.) A List of Successes That Can Change the World. LNCS, vol. 9600, pp. 169–186. Springer, Cham (2016). https://doi.org/10.1007/978-3-319-30936-1_9

Hughes, J., Norell, U., Smallbone, N., Arts, T.: Find more bugs with QuickCheck! In: Budnik, C.J., Fraser, G., Lonetti, F. (eds.) Proceedings of the 11th International Workshop on Automation of Software Test, AST@ICSE 2016, Austin, Texas, USA, 14–15 May 2016, pp. 71–77. ACM (2016)

Koopman, P.W.M., Plasmeijer, R.: Testing reactive systems with GAST. In: Gilmore, S. (ed.) Revised Selected Papers from the Fourth Symposium on Trends in Functional Programming, TFP 2003. Trends in Functional Programming, vol. 4, Edinburgh, United Kingdom, 11–12 September 2003, pp. 111–129. Intellect (2005)

Koopman, P., Plasmeijer, R.: Testing with functional reference implementations. In: Page, R., Horváth, Z., Zsók, V. (eds.) TFP 2010. LNCS, vol. 6546, pp. 134–149. Springer, Heidelberg (2011). https://doi.org/10.1007/978-3-642-22941-1_9

Koopman, P., Alimarine, A., Tretmans, J., Plasmeijer, R.: GAST: generic automated software testing. In: Peña, R., Arts, T. (eds.) IFL 2002. LNCS, vol. 2670, pp. 84–100. Springer, Heidelberg (2003). https://doi.org/10.1007/3-540-44854-3_6

Koopman, P., Achten, P., Plasmeijer, R.: Model based testing with logical properties versus state machines. In: Gill, A., Hage, J. (eds.) IFL 2011. LNCS, vol. 7257, pp. 116–133. Springer, Heidelberg (2012). https://doi.org/10.1007/978-3-642-34407-7_8

Midtgaard, J., Møller, A.: Quickchecking static analysis properties. In: Fraser, G., Marinov, D. (eds.) 8th IEEE International Conference on Software Testing, Verification and Validation, ICST 2015, Graz, Austria, April 2015, pp. 1–10. IEEE Computer Society (2015)

Midtgaard, J., Justesen, M.N., Kasting, P., Nielson, F., Nielson, H.R.: Effect-driven quickchecking of compilers. PACMPL 1(ICFP), 15:1–15:23 (2017)

Morrison, D.R.: PATRICIA–practical algorithm to retrieve information coded in alphanumeric. J. ACM 15(4), 514–534 (1968)

Nilsson, R.: ScalaCheck: The Definitive Guide. Artima, Mountain View (2014)

Okasaki, C., Gill, A.: Fast mergeable integer maps. In: Morrisett, G. (ed.) ML 1998: Proceedings of the 1998 ACM SIGPLAN Workshop on ML, pp. 77–86, September 1998

Pałka, M.H., Claessen, K., Russo, A., Hughes, J.: Testing an optimising compiler by generating random lambda terms. In: Proceedings of the 6th International Workshop on Automation of Software Test, AST 2011, pp. 91–97 (2011)

Pike, L.: SmartCheck: automatic and efficient counterexample reduction and generalization. In: Swierstra, W. (ed.) Proceedings of the 2014 ACM SIGPLAN Symposium on Haskell, Gothenburg, Sweden, 4–5 September 2014, pp. 53–64 (2014)

Reynolds, J.C.: Definitional interpreters for higher-order programming languages. In: Proceedings of the 25th ACM National Conference, Boston, Massachusetts, pp. 717–740 (1972). Reprinted in Higher-Order and Symbolic Computation 11(4), 363–397, 1998, with a foreword Reynolds (1998)

Reynolds, J.C.: Definitional interpreters revisited. Hig.-Order Symb. Comput. 11(4), 355–361 (1998)

Sergey, I.: Experience report: growing and shrinking polygons for random testing of computational geometry algorithms. In: Garrigue, J., Keller, G., Sumii, E. (eds.) Proceedings of the 21st ACM SIGPLAN International Conference on Functional Programming (ICFP 2016), pp. 193–199 (2016)

St-Amour, V., Toronto, N.: Experience report: applying random testing to a base type environment. In: Morrisett, G., Uustalu, T. (eds.) Proceedings of the 18th ACM SIGPLAN International Conference on Functional Programming (ICFP 2013), Boston, MA, pp. 351–356, September 2013

Elmsvuur: A Multi-tier Version of Elm and its Time-Traveling Debugger

Jeff Horemans, Bob Reynders[✉], Dominique Devriese, and Frank Piessens

imec-DistriNet, KU Leuven, 3001 Leuven, Belgium
horemansjeff@gmail.com,
{bob.reynders,dominique.devriese,frank.piessens}@cs.kuleuven.be

Abstract. Debugging dynamic web applications is challenging in many ways. Applications intrinsically consist of (at least) a server and a client program, each deployed on different nodes. Because of that, web applications behave like distributed systems and debugging them faces much of the same problems like managing state and heterogeneity of nodes. For web applications the latter problem also applies for the distinction between client and server code. These sections are typically written in different languages which further complicates the debugging of a web application.

The most common solution is dealing with each program layer individually using language-specific debugging tools, but this does not give an overview of the entire application flow.

Multi-tier languages allow programming a web application in a single language as a single application. They are primarily designed to offer advantages with regards to developing web applications, but this opens up new possibilities for debugging as well. We propose Elmsvuur, a multi-tier version of Elm, and a time-travel debugger for it. The debugger operates as a single tool for the whole client/server application. We discuss how advanced timeline debugging features, such as resuming from different points in the history, allows programmers to find bugs across tiers.

1 Introduction

Debugging dynamic web applications is challenging in many ways. Applications consist of (at least) a server and a client program, each deployed on different nodes with client and server often written in different languages. This variety in programming languages further complicates the debugging of a web application and makes it difficult to maintain a global view of the application when finding bugs.

Multi-tier Languages. The classical process of developing a web application consists of writing programs for the different programming layers or "tiers" of the application as well as (parts of) the logic for communication that needs to happen between them. With JavaScript being the most widely used language for client applications and various options for the other layers, they are mostly written in

© Springer International Publishing AG, part of Springer Nature 2018
M. Wang and S. Owens (Eds.): TFP 2017, LNCS 10788, pp. 79–97, 2018.
https://doi.org/10.1007/978-3-319-89719-6_5

different languages. Such applications may also require code that handles sending and receiving information between programming layers, as well as converting that information to a format that both parties can understand.

Multi-tier languages were created to solve some of these problems. They provide a developer with one language to create web applications, without the need to write programs for each layer in different languages. Instead, the code for the programming layers underneath is generated by the multi-tier framework based on the multi-tier application source code. Links [1] and Hop [2] were among the first multi-tier languages to be created, with Ur/Web [3], Hop.js [4] and Eliom [5] as more recent examples. Having only one source language means that the programming process is less partitioned, and depending on the design of the multi-tier language they can also offer various abstractions, most notably in terms of communication.

For debugging, similar simplifications apply. Multi-tier languages make it possible to have a single debugging tool for the whole application, in contrast to debuggers for each programming layer. Such tools, like the Hop debugger [6], also have the benefit of having access to the complete execution of the application.

Time Travel Debugging. Finding and resolving bugs often comes down to retracing a series of events that led to the bug. This can be quite repetitive work, especially if testing many different scenarios with the same event history. A technique that can aid in such situations is time travel debugging [7,8]. This style of debugging makes it possible to travel through the history of the application and inspect it at previous points in the execution time line directly. Other features can be: pausing the application, replaying past events (possibly with hot-swapped code), continuing from a previous point, and more.

To make this all possible, time-travel debuggers need to store some kind of information about the state of the program for each point in the timeline and about the event that caused it. Not only to be examined afterwards, but also to potentially rerun events.

Multi-tier Time Travel Debugging. We propose to combine the technique of time travel debugging with a multi-tier debugger for web applications. This combination results in a debugger that has more insight in the execution of the application because of its multi-tier nature and has time travel capabilities that apply on a multi-tier level. To accomplish this though, there are some challenges to consider.

- Multi-tier languages offer one language to develop applications, but once deployed, they consist of different programs for the server and each client like any other web application, with each of those programs having their own timeline of events. So inherently a multi-tier time travel debugger needs to deal with multiple timelines and their interaction, distributed over client and server. Figure 1 shows these different timelines with every node representing an event. It also shows how the global timeline of the application is composed out of those client and server timelines and how some of their events

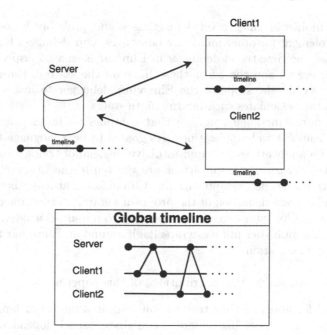

Fig. 1. Concept of multiple timelines

can be interconnected. In that context, it is important to consider how the debugger constructs that global timeline and how time travel functionalities are implemented with that architecture.

- Altering the global timeline of the application means potentially altering each of the individual timelines and their state. This process requires that after the change, the states of the server and clients end up in a consistent state.
- When the application is paused, the debugger needs to deal with events that can still be received from pending client-server communication or finishing side-effects.
- After changing the timeline of the application, events can be received that originated from a previous timeline and have no place in the new one. So the debugger has to be able to discard those accordingly.

Multi-tier Time Travel Debugging: an Implementation for Elm. Certain program architectures lend themselves better for certain styles of debugging than others, the design of a programming language or framework can largely affect how easy a debugger is constructed and used. In this paper we focus on a multi-tier debugger specific to Elmsvuur[1], our own multi-tier framework based on the Elm language [9] that lends itself well to event inspection. In fact, we point out that our design and implementation are rather specific to Elmsvuur and its architecture and the

---

[1] Elmsvuur is the dutch name for St. Elmo's fire: a weather phenomenon that produces electric discharges from sharp objects (like ship masts) in certain atmospheric conditions. The discharges remind us of messages escaping a single tier's boundary.

approach of multi-tier time-travel debugging would probably be considerably harder to implement for other multi-tier languages. Our debugger has the same design goals as the time travel debugger in Elm[2]. It is easy to inspect incoming and outgoing events and the effect these have on the state of the application but it is not within the scope of the Elmsvuur debugger to inspect the pure computation that calculates such intermediate states.

Elm is a pure functional language that compiles to JavaScript, meant for developing client-side web applications. Its goal is to be a language that makes developing web applications easy and intuitive, instead of trying to solve short-comings of JavaScript. Elm applications are written in the Elm architecture, a simple pattern for developing applications. Elm enforces at least the main module to have a separate definition of the program's state, user interface and event processing logic. Elmsvuur extends this pattern to a multi-tier level. Its debugger, written as a multi-tier library, wraps itself around an Elmsvuur application to add its instrumentation.

Overview. To summarize, the contributions of this paper are:

- A proposal for applying time-travel debugging in a multi-tier language, taking into account issues like separate timelines, causal dependencies across timelines and the interplay between events and timeline modifications.
- The design and implementation of Elmsvuur, a multi-tier version of Elm, built around a multi-tier version of the Elm architecture.
- A complete prototype implementation of both Elmsvuur and its debugger, demonstrating their practicality[3].

The remainder of this paper consists first of a look at the architecture of Elm and Elmsvuur in Sect. 2. Then we give an overview of the Elmsvuur debugger and its functionality in Sect. 3. Next, Sect. 4 offers a closer look at the architecture and design of the debugger. Next, we discuss future work in Sect. 5 followed by a final rundown of our contributions in Sect. 6 and finally conclude with related work in Sect. 7.

2   Multi-tier Elm

Elmsvuur is a natural extension of the Elm architecture to a client/server setting. Let us first look at the Elm architecture and then its multi-tier variant.

2.1   The Elm Architecture

Basic. Elm requires that every application is structured according to the Elm architecture, shown schematically in Fig. 2. In its most basic form, there are

---

[2] http://debug.elm-lang.org/.
[3] https://github.com/JeffHoremans/elm-multitier-examples.

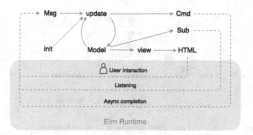

Fig. 2. The Elm architecture

three core elements: the model, the update function and the view function. The *model* is a data structure that stores the current state of the application. The *update* function is responsible for converting the current state (or model) of the application into a new one, based on an incoming message (Msg). Finally, the *view* function defines how to turn the current model into a structure representing an HTML tree. Such a structure defines what the user interface looks like as well as which input elements trigger new messages for the Elm program. The only responsibility of the programmer is to describe how to convert incoming data to outgoing data using these three elements. It is then up to the Elm runtime to connect those elements and perform actions accordingly.

Side-Effects. The basic architecture does not allow general communication and reaction to the outside world. For that, two elements are added to the basic architecture: subscriptions (Sub) and commands (Cmd). Just like the HTML construct the view generates, both are data structures that describe something for the Elm runtime to perform and both result in messages that return to the program. Subscriptions describe what Elm needs to listen to, for example a web socket or the current mouse coordinates. Commands on the other hand, describe something Elm needs to do, for example perform a HTTP request or print to the console. Effects in Elm are thus represented as data. They are not performed immediately, instead they are passed to the runtime which actually performs them while returning their results as messages for the update function.

Extensibility. The *model, update* and *view* structure is imposed on an Elm program by the main value, which is not an imperative, but a declarative main that expects a *model*, an *update* function and a *view* function. When one of those elements, or the entire main module becomes too complex, these declarations can contain declarations of sub-modules. Although not imposed, the Elm architecture is recommended to be used on those modules as well. Adding a sub-module then consists of nesting or wrapping its model, update function and view function. So even large-scale Elm applications are only composed out of those few core elements.

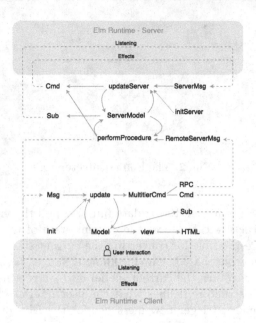

Fig. 3. The Elmsvuur architecture

2.2   The Elmsvuur Architecture

The Elmsvuur architecture in Fig. 3 extends the Elm architecture logically on a multi-tier level. Writing multi-tier applications in Elmsvuur is similar to writing regular Elm applications. Instead of requiring a three component main function, multi-tier Elm applications impose a different architecture. Although it is written as a single application, the architecture does reflect the deployment over separate Elm server and client tiers. In the following sections we explain the Elmsvuur architecture and its elements gradually.

Client Tier. In its most basic form, our Elmsvuur architecture is identical to the Elm architecture and only uses the original three core elements (model, update and view). Such a multi-tier application compiles into a default Elm server program that only hosts the simple client Elm program.

When using the full client Elm architecture with subscriptions and commands the only exception is in the type of commands. Instead of requiring `Cmd`, we require `MultitierCmd`. These new commands, can be one of two things, a regular Elm command or a remote procedure call command which we discuss later.

To summarize: the client tier is defined as a client model, a client update function and a client view function.

Server Tier. Up to this point, the resulting server program only contains default framework code to run and host the client program. To be able to extend the server application code, the Elmsvuur architecture defines server variants for each of the Elm architecture elements. The server defines its own model and update function and allows for server-side commands and subscriptions.

With the full Elm architecture on the server it would be possible to listen to the server's clock with subscriptions or write files using commands.

Asynchronous Remote Procedure Calls. The final element of the Elmsvuur architecture is the use of remote procedure calls which allow clients to perform actions on the server. These model regular HTTP requests in a multi-tier fashion and fit naturally in the asynchronous Elm architecture. They are designed as data structures that describes RPC actions and are interpreted by the Elm runtime. RPC commands may update the server model and can even result in other server commands or subscriptions. On completion, the result of the RPC is piped back to the client update cycle in the form of a message.

As mentioned above, RPCs are a type of multi-tier command but unlike regular client commands they describe something that needs to be done on the server instead of the client.

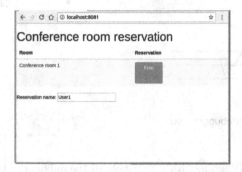

Fig. 4. Screenshot of our room reservation application.

3   Multi-tier Time Travel Debugging by Example

This section presents the Elmsvuur and its debugger using an example room reservation application. This application allows users to schedule a conference room under a given reservation name by clicking available slots. Figure 4 offers a screenshot of the application. The list of rooms with their reservations are maintained on the server, with clients performing calls for updating reservations and the server notifying clients with changes. For simplicity our interface only shows a single room and a single reservation slot. We strongly encourage the reader to explore the example and the debugger. The entire scenario as it is described here can be tested on our project[4].

To help illustrate the debugger we consider a simple scenario. Two clients try to schedule the same room and both succeed in doing so, thus exposing

---

[4] https://github.com/JeffHoremans/elm-multitier-examples

a bug. Figure 5 shows a diagram of the debugger after capturing this scenario with screenshots for the different parts of the application. In the following paragraphs we gradually explain the visual elements of the debugger and the actual debugging process.

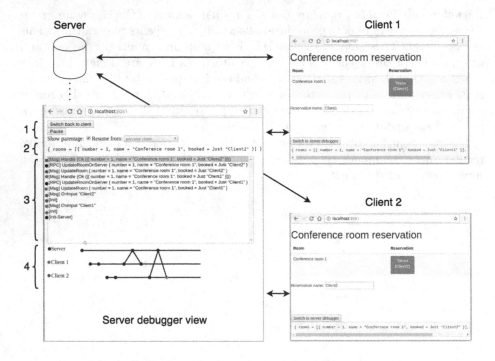

Fig. 5. Diagram with screenshots of the debugger at work.

Look and Feel. The 2 clients of the conference application are shown on the right. They are visually extended by the debugger view, by adding a data view at the bottom. It displays the current model of each client. That model contains the information about the room it is displaying, so far it has received the latest version. Additionally, there is a button above the data view, that switches the interface to the server debugger view as displayed on the left. As indicated by the dotted line, it acts as the main interface of the debugger. Client debugger views can switch back and forth to the server view for seamless debugging.

The server debugging view is composed out of roughly 4 segments, as numbered on the figure: (1) controls for various actions and configuration options, e.g., switching back to the client view, pausing and resuming, showing causal dependencies between events and setting the resume strategy – more about these later. (2) a data view of the server model (similar to the client view). In this example it contains the list of conference rooms and their information. (3) a navigable event list, containing all events from the whole client/server application which make up the global timeline with the most recent event at the top. (4) a graphical representation of this global timeline which shows extra information such as client/server communication in an intuitive way.

Debugging the Scenario: Interface. Looking at the event list (3) and the global timeline of our example (4) we can identify three types of events: initialisation events, message events and RPC events. The first represents the server or a client starting with its initial state. Message events happen when the server or a client program receives a message for the update function and RPC events describe an asynchronous client to server request. Looking at the figure, we can see that the debugger captured these events in our room reservation example. We color-coded events of a single timeline in the event list to make clear which events belong to which timeline in the global timeline.

Before looking at the scenario, we consider type definitions of a few parts of the example application in Listing 1.1. The first line contains the definition of the client model which holds the last-received list of rooms and the reservation name. On the second line, the client's messages are defined (as a union type). On lines 5 and 6, we can see the definitions of the server model and that of the room type. Finally, on line 7, remote server messages are defined, used in the asynchronous client to server RPCs. Because of the multi-tier setting, the server and client model are defined in the same code base, allowing the room type to be shared by them.

```
1 type alias Model = { rooms: List Room, name: String }
2 type Msg =
3    UpdateRoom Room | Handle (Result Error (List Room)) | OnInput String
4 ...
5 type alias ServerModel = { rooms: List Room }
6 type alias Room = { number: Int, name: String, booked: Maybe String }
7 type RemoteServerMsg = UpdateRoomOnServer Room
```

Listing 1.1. Some type definitions of our example application.

Debugging the Scenario: Identifying a Bug. The example scenario contains a bug where the room is scheduled twice. To find the bug we pause the application and use the event list and the global timeline to inspect the sequence of events. For now, it is sufficient to know that when selecting events on either of them (in 3 or 4), the data view of the server (2) and the data views of the clients output the model state at the time the event occurred.

If we look at the events sequentially, we first see the initialisation event of the server, followed by that of the first client. The latter is also visualised in the global timeline, notice that the client's timeline starts later. Next, the OnInput message is received from the DOM indicating that this client has inserted his reservation name. Then, a second client can be seen connecting and doing the same thing. After that, client 1 tries to schedule the room, triggering an UpdateRoom message on the client which updates the room with its reservation name. That message causes the UpdateRoomOnServer RPC which performs the actual reservation of the room on the server. The Handle message received on the client as a response signifies this has succeeded, containing the updated room information. Before client 2 is aware of this, he also attempts the same action and also succeeds. At that point we can see that the updating of the room on the server incorrectly overwrites the room information and does not check if it is already taken.

What this shows us, is that the bug is related to that part in our implementation. The debugger gives us a good estimate that the code that dispatches the `UpdateRoomOnServer` RPC contains a bug. This interactive inspection of the client/server program as a whole quickly allows programmers to identify bugs in sections of code.

4   Multi-tier Elm Debugger

4.1   Architecture

The Elmsvuur debugger itself is written as an Elmsvuur application, it follows the Elmsvuur architecture of Sect. 2.2. To debug other Elmsvuur applications, it wraps itself around them by extending each element of their architecture with its own. This concept is shown in Fig. 6 where each element of the debugger architecture is an extension of the instrumented application. It allows the debugger to have complete control over the application.

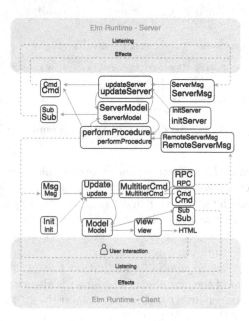

Fig. 6. The Elm multi-tier debugger architecture

Both on the server and on the client, the application model is nested in the debugger model. The debugger stores the application's model as well as additional state specific to the debugger. The top-level messages are debugger messages, so application messages are wrapped as debugger messages and first handled by the debugger update function. This allows the debugger to monitor messages before they reach the application and make it possible to store or discard them before propagating the message to the application's update function. By wrapping the view function, the debugger is able to add debugger specific sections to the interface.

4.2 Global Timeline

The most prominent feature of the debugger interface is the visualization of the global timeline. It is shown in the form of an event list and in the form of a graphical global timeline.

They both form the same interactive stepper, with each node on the graph (representing an event) in the global timeline corresponding from left to right with the event data in the list above from bottom to top. Clicking events, either in the list or on the timeline, can be used to step the application back to a previous point in the global timeline. There are two functionalities exposed by stepping back in the timeline. First, it can be used to quickly inspect different states of the server model without impacting the entire application. Secondly, if the client/server application is paused its true functionality can be used to step back through the entire application. This results in the server and *each* client updating their data view with their past model at the time of the event. For clients, this also means updating their UI to its past state. Stepping through the timeline thus allows inspecting events, but also shows how the models and views of the different parts of the applications evolved over time. The entire client/server application can be inspected as a single entity.

Event Order. An important thing to consider is the order of the timeline events. We do not rebuild a global timeline based on some notion of synchronized clocks. Instead, the debugger keeps track of a list of events in the order they are received on the server. We make some assumptions to make this practical:

- The global timeline does not give an exact reflection of the real timeline. The global timeline does not allow for events that occur at the same time. From the server's point of view, an order is enforced.
- We do not visualize the actual time in the timelines, e.g., in reality an event can take a month to occur yet it shows up right behind the last event in the timeline.

We found these assumptions to provide a good balance between reflecting the actual situation and providing a good user experience. While our approach cannot reproduce the exact global timeline, it does give an approximation that has sufficient guarantees for debugging purposes.

Note that our prototype implementation still uses common HTTP requests to send event data over the network to the server from the clients. At the moment this is an implementation bug since the order of multiple HTTP requests cannot be guaranteed to be the same as the order in which they actually occurred. This can be solved by using communication that ensures in-order delivery, such as websockets.

Pausing and Resuming. When the application is running, the models of the different tiers are kept up-to-date and the timeline is being updated with all incoming events. From the moment the application is paused, the interface of the clients is frozen. The debugger then allows quick inspection of previous states throughout the entire client/server application.

When stepping the application back to a previous point in the global timeline, the server and clients are notified to step back to their previous state at that point. For this to be possible, the debugger does not just store each event that occurs, it also keeps snapshots of the model of the server or each corresponding client. With that information, the debugger can find the latest model state for each connected client and the server whenever a point is selected to step back to.

Since we are dealing with a distributed environment, pausing and resuming the application does not happen instantly at every tier. Between the time of pausing at the server, and the client being instructed by the server to pause as well, client events can have occurred. The same applies for resuming the application. As such, in the background the application still runs and reacts to the outside world. When the application is resumed this backgrounded model is made current again and the application can seamlessly continue. This process is shown in Figs. 7 and 8.

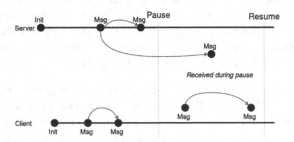

Fig. 7. Example timeline when paused

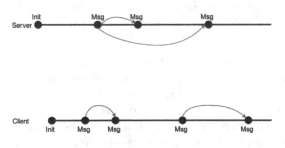

Fig. 8. Example timeline after resuming

Stepping Back and Changing the Global Timeline. The debugger not only allows quick inspection of several points in the timeline, it also allows the programmer to resume from a previous point. This can be useful to test multiple related scenarios which take many common events to set up, for instance testing different error cases in a form.

Resuming from a previous point or event in the global timeline and thereby changing it raises some important challenges:

- The debugger should be able to determine which events after the resume point need to be kept and which to be removed. Events triggered by user interaction or subscriptions need to be discarded as they are exactly the type of events we would like to change by resuming from a previous point. But, for events corresponding to side-effects this does not necessarily apply. In Elm, side-effectful code is always executed asynchronously and their results enter the program as a message. If such messages are the result of a side-effect that started before the resume point, it needs to be kept to keep all the events in the timeline consistent. The same applies for a chain of these connected events that originated before the resume point. An example of this problem is shown in Fig. 9.
- By changing the global timeline, at any point in time, events can still be received asynchronously from finishing side-effects (even from past timelines!). Some of these results may be started because of an event that has already been removed from the timeline. These results need to be detected and discarded to keep consistency.

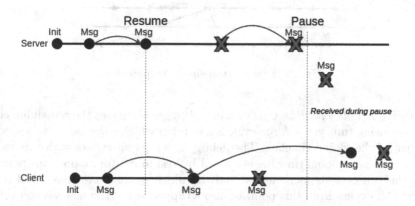

Fig. 9. Discarding events when changing the timeline

The debugger deals with these challenges using two concepts, parentage and run cycles:

Causal Dependencies: Parentage. To handle the first challenge, the debugger first needs to be able to distinguish between events that were caused by user interaction, by subscriptions or indirectly by side-effects from processing other events. It does so by wrapping message events triggered in the view, by subscriptions or by commands appropriately. This already allows discarding the first two types of events properly. Whenever the timeline resumes from a certain point, all events that originated from HTML (the view) and subscriptions are discarded immediately. But for the last type we need more information to determine if it should be discarded or not. For those events we need to be able to check if they are part of an event chain that originated before the resume point or after. This is where the concept 'parentage' comes into play.

For this, the debugger keeps track of direct relations between events. In Elm side-effectful code returns its results asynchronously in the form of a message. By wrapping that message definition with a reference to the event that caused it, it becomes possible to figure out where these messages originated from. Using this reference, we can later identify parent relationships between messages. With this feature, we can handle event chains properly and check if new messages need to be discarded or not. Both cases can be seen in Fig. 9 that shows an example discarding process with parent relations visualised.

Since the debugger keeps track of these causal dependencies anyway, we decided to visualize them using arcs in the timeline. In Fig. 10, we include a small screenshot of a global timeline with this feature enabled. From our experience, this functionality is useful for users to get a better understanding of how events are related.

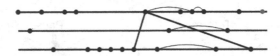

Fig. 10. Example timeline with parentage

Discarding Events with Run Cycles. The debugger addresses the remaining challenges by using run cycles. A run cycle is a number which corresponds to a specific instance of the global timeline. The debugger wraps all events with this value. Whenever a new global timeline is started by resuming from a previous point in time, the run cycle is incremented and the older versions are considered to be invalid. All events from this point on are wrapped using the new version of the number.

Figure 11 shows how we can use run cycles to discard the proper events. The program is run (cycle 0) and is paused before a final asynchronous side-effect has finished computing (pending (0)). We resume the application from a previous point (the second Msg on the client) which creates a new run cycle (1). We now have two pending asynchronous side-effects belonging to two different run cycles. The current run cycle is 1, as such, whenever pending (0) finishes computing its messages are discarded.

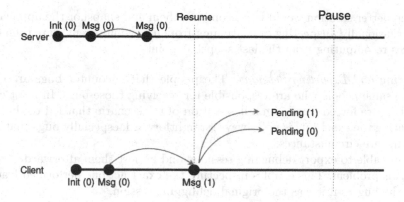

Fig. 11. Using run cycles when rerunning events

Invalidating Clients. When changing the global timeline it is possible to rewind all the way back to a point where clients did not yet exist. In this case these clients need to be invalidated since they should not have been created yet. The timeline of such clients is completely removed from the debugger interface and a message indicating their invalidation is shown on the clients. An example can be seen in Fig. 12. The client can still be used as an interface to the server debugger interface, but a refresh is required to start a new client session.

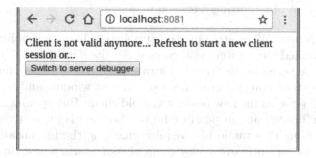

Fig. 12. Screenshot of an invalidated client

5   Future Work

More Efficient Snapshots. The debugger stores data for each incoming event, including a snapshot with the current state of the application. When debugging for long periods of time, this amount of data can grow large and eventually make the debugger too slow. Using the alternative method of recomputing the program state instead of storing it does requires less space, but will grow in computation time instead.

The better solution would be to combine them and snapshot the application only occasionally. Inspecting or continuing from a previous event state then only requires recomputing from the last snapshot point.

Importing and Exporting Sessions. The people that encounter bugs are often not the same people who are responsible for resolving those bugs. In most cases the latter are forced to rely on a description of the scenario that led to the bug. Recreating the exact bug is not always straightforward, especially bugs that only occur in rare circumstances.

Being able to export debugging sessions and import them afterwards, would solve this problem. This enables inspecting the exact actions performed leading up to the bug as if it was the original debugging session.

Importing sessions has some requirements though. When importing a session, the program may already be altered, possibly making it impossible to import the session. It would be necessary to detect if the session that is to be imported is still consistent with the current program.

Hot Swapping. The debugger currently does not allow for hot swapping modified code. As a result, checking if a bug is resolved after making changes requires restarting the debugger and the debugging scenario that caused the bug.

Having the feature of importing and exporting sessions, discussed in the previous paragraph, could offer a partial solution. The debugger could then export the debugging session with the bug, restart using the modified program and import the session again for retesting the bug. But this only works if the consistency requirement of importing a session is met.

Client Resurrection. When stepping the application back to a point where currently disconnected clients were still connected, the debugger has no means to restart them. A potential resurrection strategy could be to let the client that is operating as the debugger interface, open a new window and start a special client who will serve as the new host for the old client. But opening new browser windows with JavaScript can possibly be blocked and is currently not natively supported in Elm. This would also require changing the initialisation phase of the debugger, as currently every new client session starts a new timeline.

A simpler option would be to extend the debugger interface and allow switching to resurrected clients in the same client window, which solves the remarks of the previous approach. The server already keeps track of client connections, so when it detects trying to contact a disconnected client, it can reroute the information to the clients who are operating as the debugger interface.

Visualising WebSocket Communication. Elmsvuur supports two kinds of communication between client-server: RPC communication and WebSocket communication. The first of which is already visualised in the global timeline of its debugger. RPC communication is controlled on both ends by Elmsvuur and is a part of its multi-tier architecture. This allows them to be extended by the debugger to include the parent information that is needed to visualize the communication.

To do the same for WebSockets communication, it also would need to become part of the multi-tier architecture. We use the existing Elm WebSocket library on the client, and a custom written server library on the server, both using regular commands and subscriptions to expose their functionality. A possible solution would be to build a construct that builds on those libraries, similar to the RPC construct building on top of the Elm HTTP library.

6   Conclusion

In this paper we propose a multi-tier debugger, a tool that can be used to debug an entire client/server application as a single entity. It focuses on web applications that are written using multi-tier languages, that is, web applications that originate from a single codebase but are deployed to both client and server. The debugger experience is focused on providing an interactive global timeline for the application as a whole. We propose complex features with an intuitive interface that allows programmers to quickly observe different states of a client/server web application, as well as resume from any point in time.

To make our ideas more concrete we created a multi-tier version of the Elm language. The multi-tier language uses an extended version of the Elm architecture. We created the multi-tier debugger not as a low-level tool that inspects Elm programs but as a high-level multi-tier Elm library that wraps multi-tier applications with instrumentation as needed.

We succeeded in creating a prototype that demonstrates complex features such as being able to inspect different states of a distributed application as a whole as well as resume from earlier points in the history. We identified and solved non-trivial issues such as dealing with asynchronous effects.

7   Related Work

We consider mainly work on time-travel debugging, distributed debugging and specifically, multi-tier web application debugging.

Time-Travel Debugging. We can roughly divide time-travel debuggers into two classes. One builds its timeline by capturing the application's state (e.g. ODB [8]), others capture out and incoming calls to the application (e.g. AIDS debugger for FORTRAN [10] or [7] for SML). Liblog [11] is a replay debugging tool for distributed C/C++ applications. It captures the execution of deployed distributed applications and replays them deterministically. For the browser, Dolos [12] captures out and incoming calls to the application for the browser engine, including user inputs and network callbacks.

The examples of these approaches are implemented as low-level tools and intercept system calls or other low level operations (such as calls to libc). In contrast, Elmsvuur is implemented as a library that wraps its target. Elm, a pure language, allows us to make some assumptions which makes this both easier and elegant. In our implementation we capture both the application's state as well as the out and incoming calls to the application. Other than just its history functionality, our tool focuses on providing a pleasant user experience with easy-to-understand timeline graphics and other visuals.

Distributed Debugging and Causal Dependencies. Causeway [13] takes a message-oriented approach and builds what they call 'chains of expressed intentions'. Such a chain is a path of a (possibly distributed) computation, akin to a high-level stack trace it displays the causal dependencies between events and the processing thereof. We employ a concept similar to chains in our debugger to graphically show users which events trigger as a direct result of other events. For example, executing an RPC command on the client graphically shows a connection between that client's view of the timeline and the server's.

Multi-tier Debugging. In academic work the Hop debugger [6] copes with both server and client-side executions. Their debugger focuses on providing a single-application overview for all stack traces. Errors and their traces report the correct source-code location regardless of whether the error occurred on the client or the server. Albeit with a completely different debugging experience, similarly to Hop, we treat a client/server application as a single entity to debug.

In industry the Google Web Toolkit (GWT) project is the only multi-tier language that considers debugging. GWT is a Java-based multi-tier language that runs its server side on the JVM and compiles Java to JavaScript for client code. It can run in production mode or in dev-mode. Dev-mode does not compile the client code to JavaScript, instead it runs it as a Java application while propagating changes to a browser application. In this mode Java tools can be used to debug both tiers of an application, however, the client/server application is still seen as two entities to debug.

Acknowledgements. Bob Reynders holds an SB fellowship of the Research Foundation - Flanders (FWO). Dominique Devriese holds a postdoctoral fellowship of the Research Foundation - Flanders (FWO). This research is partially funded by the Research Fund KU Leuven, and by the SBO-project TearLess.

References

1. Cooper, E., Lindley, S., Wadler, P., Yallop, J.: Links: web programming without tiers. In: de Boer, F.S., Bonsangue, M.M., Graf, S., de Roever, W.-P. (eds.) FMCO 2006. LNCS, vol. 4709, pp. 266–296. Springer, Heidelberg (2007). https://doi.org/10.1007/978-3-540-74792-5_12
2. Serrano, M., Gallesio, E., Loitsch, F.: Hop: a language for programming the web 2.0. In: DLS, pp. 975–985 (2006)
3. Chlipala, A.: Ur/Web. In: POPL, pp. 153–165 (2015)
4. Serrano, M., Prunet, V.: A glimpse of Hopjs. In: ICFP (2016)
5. Radanne, G., Vouillon, J., Balat, V.: ELIOM: a core ML language for tierless web programming. In: Igarashi, A. (ed.) APLAS 2016. LNCS, vol. 10017, pp. 377–397. Springer, Cham (2016). https://doi.org/10.1007/978-3-319-47958-3_20

6. Serrano, M.: A multitier debugger for web applications. In: WEBIST, pp. 5–16 (2014)
7. Tolmach, A., Appel, A.W.: A debugger for standard ML. J. Funct. Program. 5(2), 155–200 (1995)
8. Lewis, B.: Debugging backwards in time. In: AADEBUG (2003)
9. Czaplicki, E., Chong, S.: Asynchronous functional reactive programming for GUIs. In: PLDI, pp. 411–422 (2013)
10. Grishman, R.: The debugging system AIDS. In: Proceedings of the 5–7 May 1970, Spring Joint Computer Conference, AFIPS 1970 (Spring), pp. 59–64. ACM (1970)
11. Geels, D., Altekar, G., Shenker, S., Stoica, I.: Replay debugging for distributed applications. In: USENIX, pp. 289–300 (2006)
12. Burg, B., Bailey, R., Ko, A.J., Ernst, M.D.: Interactive record/replay for web application debugging. In: UIST, pp. 473–484. ACM (2013)
13. Stanley, T., Close, T., Miller, M.S.: Causeway: a message-oriented distributed debugger (2009)

Concurrent System Programming
with Effect Handlers

Stephen Dolan[1], Spiros Eliopoulos[3], Daniel Hillerström[2], Anil Madhavapeddy[1],
K. C. Sivaramakrishnan[1](✉) (iD), and Leo White[3]

[1] University of Cambridge, Cambridge, England
sk826@cl.cam.ac.uk
[2] The University of Edinburgh, Edinburgh, Scotland
[3] Jane Street Group, New York City, USA

Abstract. Algebraic effects and their handlers have been steadily gain-
ing attention as a programming language feature for composably expressing user-defined computational effects. While several prototype implementations of languages incorporating algebraic effects exist, Multicore
OCaml incorporates effect handlers as the primary means of expressing
concurrency in the language. In this paper, we make the observation that
effect handlers can elegantly express particularly difficult programs that
combine system programming and concurrency without compromising
performance. Our experimental results on a highly concurrent and scalable web server demonstrate that effect handlers perform on par with
highly optimised monadic concurrency libraries, while retaining the simplicity of direct-style code.

1 Introduction

Algebraic effect handlers are a modular foundation for effectful programming,
which separate the *operations* available to effectful programs from their concrete implementations as *handlers*. Effect handlers provide a modular alternative to monads [25,35] for structuring effectful computations. They achieve
the separation between operations and their handlers through the use of delimited continuations, allowing them to pause, resume and switch between different
computations. They provide a structured interface for programming with delimited continuations [10], and can implement common abstractions such as state,
generators, async/await, promises, non-determinism, exception handlers and
backtracking search. Though originally studied in a theoretical setting [27,28],
effect handlers have gained practical interest with several prototype implementations in the form of libraries, interpreters, compilers and runtime representations [4,5,9,12,15,16,20,21].

However, the application space of effect handlers remains largely unexplored.
In this paper we explore the applicability of effect handlers to concurrent system
programming in Multicore OCaml. While Multicore OCaml supports shared-
memory parallel programming, this paper restricts its focus to concurrency i.e.
overlapped execution of tasks, leaving parallelism outside our scope.

© Springer International Publishing AG, part of Springer Nature 2018
M. Wang and S. Owens (Eds.): TFP 2017, LNCS 10788, pp. 98–117, 2018.
https://doi.org/10.1007/978-3-319-89719-6_6

2   Motivation

Multicore OCaml [8] incorporates effect handlers as the primary means of expressing concurrency in the language. The modular nature of effect handlers allows the concurrent program to abstract over different scheduling strategies [9]. Moreover, effect handlers allow concurrent programs to be written in *direct-style* retaining the simplicity of sequential code as opposed to callback-oriented style (as used by e.g. Lwt [34] and Async [24]). In addition to being more read-able, direct-style code tends to be easier to debug; unlike callback-oriented code, direct-style code uses the stack for function calls, and hence, backtraces can be obtained for debugging. Indeed, experience from Google suggests that as well as making the code more compact and easier to understand (particularly important when thousands of developers touch the code), direct-style code can perform as well or better than callback-oriented code [3].

Some of the benefits of direct-style code can be achieved by rewriting direct-style functions into callbacks, using syntactic sugar such as Haskell's do-notation for monads or F#'s `async/await` [32]. However, this separates functions which use such rewriting from those that do not, leading to awkward mismatches and code duplication: for instance, Haskell provides `mapM, filterM` and `foldM` because the ordinary `map, filter` and `foldl` functions do not work with monadic arguments. By contrast, effect handlers do not introduce an incompatible type of function.

In Multicore OCaml, the user-level thread schedulers themselves are expressed as OCaml libraries, thus minimising the secret sauce that gets baked into high-performance multicore runtime systems [31]. This modular design allows the scheduling policy to be changed by swapping out the scheduler library for a different one with the same interface. As the scheduler is a library, it can live outside the compiler distribution and be tailored to application requirements.

However, the interaction between user-level threading systems and the oper-ating system services is difficult. For example, the Unix `write()` system call may block if the underlying buffer is full. This would be fine in a sequential program or a program with each user-level thread mapped to a unique OS thread, but with many user-level threads multiplexed over a single OS thread, a blocking system call blocks the entire program. How then can we safely allow interaction between user-level threads and system services?

Concurrent Haskell [23], which also has user-level threads, solves the prob-lem with the help of specialised runtime system features such as safe FFI calls and bound threads. However, implementing these features in the runtime system warrants that the scheduler itself be part of the runtime system, which is incom-patible with our goal of writing thread schedulers in OCaml. Attempts to lift the scheduler from the runtime system to a library in the high-level language while retaining other features in the runtime system lead to further complications [31]. Our goals then are:

- Retain the simplicity of direct-style code for concurrent OCaml programs.
- Allow user-level thread schedulers to be written in OCaml as libraries.
- Allow safe interaction between user-level threads and the operating system.

– Perform as well as or better than existing solutions.

We observe that algebraic effects and their handlers can meet all of these goals. In particular, we introduce *asynchronous effects* and their handlers, and show how they elegantly solve the interaction between user-level threads and operating system services. This paper makes the following contributions:

– We introduce effect handlers for Multicore OCaml and illustrate their utility by constructing a high-performance asynchronous I/O library that exposes a direct style API (Sect. 3).
– We show how *asynchronous effects* provide a clean interface to difficult-to-use operating system services, such as signal handling and asynchronous notification of I/O completion, and demonstrate how effect handlers enable scoped interrupt handling (Sect. 4).
– We evaluate the performance of effect handlers in OCaml by implementing a highly scalable web server and show that Multicore OCaml effect handlers are efficient (Sect. 5).

After the technical content of the paper in Sects. 3, 4, and 5, we discuss related work in Sect. 6 and our conclusions in Sect. 7.

3   Algebraic Effects and Their Handlers

Since the primary motivation for adding effect handlers in Multicore OCaml is concurrency, we introduce effect handlers in constructing an asynchronous I/O library which retains the simplicity of direct-style programming[1].

3.1   Concurrency

We start with an abstraction for creating asynchronous tasks and waiting on their results. We use the term *fiber* to indicate a lightweight user-level thread to distinguish it from kernel threads.

```
val async : (α → β) → α → β promise
(* [async f v] spawns a fiber to run [f v] asynchronously. *)

val await : α promise → α
(* Block until the result of a promise is available. Raises
   exception [e] if the promise raises [e]. *)

val yield : unit → unit
(* Yield control to other fibers. *)
```

Multicore OCaml extends OCaml with the ability to declare user-defined effects with the help of the `effect` keyword. Since `async`, `await` and `yield` are effectful operations, we declare them as follows:

---

[1] A comprehensive list of example programs written using effect handlers in Multicore OCaml is available at https://github.com/kayceesrk/effects-examples.

```
effect Async : (α → β) * α → β promise
effect Await : α promise → α
effect Yield : unit
```

The first declaration says that `Async` is an effect which is parameterised by a pair of a thunk and a value, and returns a promise as a result when performed. `Await` is parameterised by a promise and returns the result. `Yield` is a nullary effect that returns a unit value. To be precise, these declarations are *operations* of a single built-in effect type α `eff` in Multicore OCaml. Indeed, these declarations are syntactic sugar for extending the built-in extensible variant type α `eff`:

```
type _ eff +=
  | Async : (α → β) * α → β promise eff
  | Await : α promise → α eff
  | Yield : unit eff
```

Effects are performed with the `perform` :α `eff` → α primitive, which performs the effect and returns the result. We can now define the functions `async`, `await` and `yield` as:

```
let async f v = perform (Async (f,v))
let await p   = perform (Await p)
let yield () = perform Yield
```

These effects are interpreted by an effect handler, as shown in Fig. 1. A promise (lines 1–6) is either completed successfully `Done` v, failed with an exception `Error` e or still pending `Waiting` l, with a list of fibers waiting on it for completion. The function `run` (line 8) is the top-level function that runs the `main` concurrent program. `run_q` is the queue of concurrent fibers ready to run. The effect handler itself is defined in the lines 17–38. An effect handler comprises of five clauses – a value clause, an exception clause, and three clauses that handle the effects `Async`, `Await` and `Yield`.

Effect clauses are of the form `effect e k` where e is the effect and k is the continuation of the corresponding `perform` delimited by this handler. k is of type (α ,β) `continuation`, representing a continuation waiting for a value of type α and returning a value of type β when resumed. There are two primitives operating on continuations: `continue k x` resumes the continuation k where it left off, returning the value x from `perform`, while `discontinue k exn` resumes the continuation k by raising the exception exn from `perform`.

In the case of an `Async` (f,v) effect (lines 28–31), we create a new promise value p which is initially waiting to be completed. We set up the original fibers, represented by continuation k, to resume with the promise using the `continue` primitive. Finally, we recursively call `fork` to run the new fiber f v. Since Multicore OCaml uses so-called *deep handlers*, the continuation k references its surrounding handler, and so we need not write another `match` expression when `continue`-ing k (See Kammar et al. [15] for more on deep vs. shallow handlers).

In the case of `Await` p, we check whether the promise is complete. If successful, we immediately resume with the value, and if failed, we use the `discontinue` primitive to resume the continuation by raising an exception. Otherwise, we

```
1  type α _promise = Done of α | Error of exn
2                         | Waiting of (α, unit) continuation list
3
4  type α promise = α _promise ref
5
6  let run main v =
7    let run_q = Queue.create () in
8    let enqueue f = Queue.push f run_q in
9    let run_next () =
10     if Queue.is_empty run_q then ()
11     else Queue.pop run_q ()
12   in
13   let rec fork : α β. α promise → (β → α) → β → unit =
14     fun p f v →
15       match f v with
16       | v →
17           let Waiting l = !p in
18           List.iter (fun k →
19             enqueue (fun () → continue k v)) l;
20           p ≔ Done v;
21           run_next ()
22       | exception e →
23           let Waiting l = !p in
24           List.iter (fun k →
25             enqueue (fun () → discontinue k e)) l;
26           p ≔ Error e;
27           run_next ()
28       | effect (Async (f,v)) k →
29           let p = ref (Waiting []) in
30           enqueue (fun () → continue k p);
31           fork p f v
32       | effect (Await p) k →
33           match !p with
34           | Done v → continue k v
35           | Error e → discontinue k e
36           | Waiting l → p ≔ Waiting (k::l); run_next ()
37       | effect Yield k →
38           enqueue (fun () → continue k ());
39           run_next ()
40     in
41   fork (ref (Waiting [])) main v
```

Fig. 1. A simple scheduler, implemented with effects

block the current fiber on the promise and resume the next fiber from the scheduler. In the case of Yield effect, we enqueue the current fiber and run the next available fiber. In the case of a fiber successfully running to completion (lines 18–23) or raising an exception (lines 24–29), we update the promise, wake up the waiting fibers and resume the next available fiber.

3.2   Implementing Effect Handlers

Unlike other languages that incorporate effect handlers, effects in Multicore OCaml are unchecked. That is, there is no static check for whether all the possible effects have been handled in the program. As a result, a fiber that performs an unhandled effect is discontinued with `Unhandled` exception.

There are several alternatives to implement the continuations in effect handlers including free monadic interpretations [16,17,36], CPS translations [13,20], and runtime strategies. Multicore OCaml chooses the latter and uses a custom stack layout, efficiently supported by the runtime system. We observe that many effect handlers do not resume the continuations more than once, and support only linear continuations by default, which can be implemented efficiently [9]. We also support explicit copying for non-linear use of continuations.

3.3   Adding I/O

Next let us add support for the following I/O operations:

```
val accept : file_descr → file_descr * sockaddr
val recv : file_descr → bytes → int → int
        → msg_flag list → int
val send : file_descr → bytes → int → int
        → msg_flag list → int
```

These functions have the *same* signature as their counterparts in the `Unix` module. However, invoking any of these functions may block the kernel thread until the I/O operation is complete. In a user-level threaded system this would block the scheduler, preventing other fibers from running.

The standard solution to this problem is to use an event loop, suspending each task performing a blocking I/O operation, and then multiplexing the outstanding I/O operations through an OS-provided blocking mechanism such as `select`, `epoll`, `kqueue`, `IOCP`, etc. Such asynchronous, non-blocking code typically warrants callback-oriented programming, making the continuations of I/O operations explicit through explicit callbacks (à la JavaScript) or concurrency monad (Lwt and Async libraries for OCaml). The resultant code is arguably messier and more difficult to understand than direct-style code.

Effect handlers lets us retain direct-style while still allowing the use of event loops. Below, we shall just consider `accept`. The other functions are similar. As earlier, we start by declaring an effect for an `accept` function: `effect Accept : file_descr → (file_descr * sockaddr)`. The handler for `Accept` is:

```
| effect (Accept fd) k →
    (match Unix.accept fd with
    | (newfd, sockaddr) →
        continue k (newfd, sockaddr)
    | exception Unix_error(EWOULDBLOCK, _, _) →
        record_waiting fd k; run_next ())
```

If there is a waiting connection, `Unix.accept` returns it and we resume the continuation. If not, `Unix.accept` raises the `EWOULDBLOCK` error, and we record that the fiber is waiting to accept and switch to the next thread from the scheduler queue. The `send` and `recv` operations have similar handler implementations.

```
let run_next () =
  if Queue.is_empty run_q then
    if io_is_pending () then begin
      wait_until_io_ready (); do_io (); run_next ()
    end else () (* done *)
  else Queue.pop run_q ()
```

Correspondingly, the `run_next` function is updated such that it first runs all the available threads, and then if any I/O is pending it waits until at least one of the I/O operations is ready, and then tries to perform the I/O and continue. If the scheduler queue is empty, and there is no pending I/O, then the scheduler returns. The library blocks on I/O only if there are no ready threads and there are pending I/O operations.

Using this API, we can write a simple server that echoes client messages:

```
let rec echo_server sock =
  let sent = ref 0 in
  let msg_len = (* receive message *)
    try recv sock buffer 0 buf_size [] with
    | _ → 0 (* Treat exceptions as 0 length message *) in
  if msg_len > 0 then begin
    (* echo message *)
    (try while !sent < msg_len do
      let write_count =
        send sock buffer !sent (msg_len - !sent) [] in
      sent = write_count + !sent
    done with _ → ()); (* ignore send failures *)
    echo_server sock
  end else close sock (* client left, close connection *)
```

The details of the code are not important, but observe that the code is in direct-style and moreover is the *same* code for the synchronous, blocking echo server. Furthermore, since the following code is asynchronous, the two echo servers on `sock1` and `sock2` do not block each other:

```
run (fun () →
    async echo_server sock1; async echo_server sock2) ()
```

3.4 Default Handlers

For an invocation of an effectful operation to be meaningful it must happen in the scope of an appropriate handler. A default handler is a convenient mechanism for ensuring that an operation invocation is always meaningful even when not in scope of a handler. A default handler provides a *default* interpretation of an operation. This interpretation is chosen if no other appropriate handler encloses the invocation context. In other words, a default handler can operationally be understood as a top level handler which encloses the entire program context including itself. As a concrete example we can give a default synchronous semantics for `Accept`

```
effect Accept : file_descr → (file_descr * sockaddr)
  with function Accept fd → Unix.accept fd
```

In Multicore OCaml a default handler is declared along with the effectful operation it is handling using the familiar `function` construct. In contrast to a regular effect handler, a default handler does not expose the continuation of the operation to the programmer, rather, the continuation is implicitly applied to the body clause(s). This particular design admits an efficient implementation, since every continuation invocation in a default handler is guaranteed to be in tail position. Thus the runtime does not need to allocate a continuation, it can simply return the value produced by the default handler clause. As a consequence an invocation of a default handler amounts to a function call. This makes it possible for effectful libraries to remain *performance backwards compatible* with programs that do not use regular effect handlers.

Continuing, we can also obtain the synchronous counterparts to `Await`, `Async`, and `Yield` by giving them all a default synchronous semantics, i.e.

```
effect Async : (α → β) * α → β promise
  with function Async (f, v) →
    match f v with
    | v → ref (Done v)
    | exception e → ref (Error e)

effect Await : α promise → α
  with function Await (ref (Done v)) → v
               | Await (ref (Error e)) → raise e

effect Yield : unit with function Yield → ()
```

If a default handler raises an exception, then the fiber is discontinued with that exception. Furthermore, if a default handler performs an effect then the default handler of that effect is invoked. If we define the default implementations of `Send` and `Recv` in a similar way then by using default handlers the following program behaves exactly like its synchronous counterpart.

```
async echo_server sock1; async echo_server sock2
```

4   Programming with Resources and Effects

Systems programming generally involves the manipulation of scarce resources such as file handles, connections and locks. Such resources are inherently linear, stateful values: once a file handle is closed, it cannot be used again.

Ordinary straight-line imperative code is not enough to use resources correctly in the presence of exceptions, let alone effects. For instance, the following code leaks an unclosed file handle if `do_stuff_with f` raises an exception:

```
let f = open_in ''data.csv'' in
do_stuff_with f;
close_in f
```

We need to ensure that the file handle is closed, even if an exception is raised:

```
let f = open_in ''data.csv'' in
match do_stuff_with f with
| () → close_in f
| exception e → close_in f; raise e
```

Note that the initial open_in occurs outside the exception handler - if opening the file fails with an exception, we need not close it. This idiom or something equivalent is widespread, often with syntactic support as try-finally.

However, note an implicit assumption in this code, that if do_stuff_with f terminates then it does so only once. If the computation do_stuff_with f were to return twice (by allowing a continuation captured inside f to be resumed twice), then the cleanup code (close_in f in this example) would incorrectly run multiple times. If the computation do_stuff_with_f were to continue execution after the cleanup code had run, its operations would have unexpected effects.

As well as the performance advantages mentioned above, this is the other major reason that our continuations are linear. By preserving the linearity of computations (operations that are begun once do not complete twice), we allow resource-manipulating code to work correctly in the presence of effects.

Some interesting examples of programming with effects and handlers (such as backtracking) are incompatible with this approach, since they rely on continuations to be usable more than once. To support experimenting with such examples, we do provide a primitive to allow re-use of continuations, with the proviso that it is not safe in general when used with code that handles resources.

The linearity of computations is implicit in OCaml without effect handlers, but once continuations appear as first-class values the possibility of using them twice arises. OCaml does not have the linear types necessary to prevent this statically (and we are not proposing to add them), so we must enforce linearity dynamically. Ensuring that a continuation is not used twice is easy enough, by keeping a bit of state in the continuation, updated by continue and discontinue so that subsequent resumptions fail. Ensuring that a continuation is not simply discarded is harder: the system must detect when a continuation is being garbage-collected, and discontinue it with a special exception so that resource cleanup code runs.

4.1   Asynchronous Exceptions

Correct use of resources is much more difficult in the presence of *asynchronous exceptions*. For example, on Unix-like systems when the user of a command-line program presses Ctrl-C the SIGINT signal is sent. By default, this terminates the program. However, programs may indicate that they can handle this signal, for instance by cancelling a long-running task and accepting user input again.

In OCaml, programs indicate willingness to handle SIGINT by calling
Sys.catch_break true. From that point onwards, the special exception Sys.Break
may be raised at essentially any point in the program, if the user presses Ctrl-C.
Unfortunately, the try-finally idiom does not clean up correctly in this case:

```
let f = open_in ''data.csv'' in
match do_stuff_with f with
| () → close_in f
| exception e → close_in f; raise e
```

If Sys.Break is raised just after open_in returns but before the match statement
is entered, then the file handle will never be closed. To eliminate this possibility,
we need to temporarily disable asynchronous exceptions. Suppose we introduce
two functions set_mask and clear_mask, to disable (*mask*) and re-enable asynchronous exceptions. Our second attempt at resource handling looks like:

```
set_mask ();
let f = open_in ''data.csv'' in
match clear_mask (); do_stuff_with f; set_mask () with
| () → close_in f; clear_mask ()
| exception e → set_mask (); close_in f; clear_mask ();
    raise e
```

Correctly placing calls to set_mask and clear_mask is a very tricky business.
Indeed, the above code has a serious bug: if open_in fails with an ordinary
synchronous exception (because e.g. the file is not found), then asynchronous
exceptions will never be unmasked.

Instead, we follow the good advice of Marlow et al. in the design of Haskell's
asynchronous exceptions [22], and prefer instead *scoped combinators*:

```
mask (fun () →
  let f = open_in ''data.csv'' in
  match unmask (fun () → do_stuff_with f) with
  | () → close_in f
  | exception e → close_in f; raise e)
```

The changes to the masking state made by mask and unmask apply only to
one scope, and are automatically undone, making it impossible to accidentally
leave asynchronous exceptions masked. The presence of unmask allows a further
improvement to the semantics: we model the asynchronous exception Sys.Break
as being raised not by whatever code happened to be executing when Ctrl-C was
pressed, but by the nearest enclosing unmask. This ensures that exception handlers for asynchronous exceptions need not be treated specially. In particular,
the follow code cannot fail, no matter when Ctrl-C is pressed:

```
match 1 + 1 with
| n → n
| exception Sys.Break → failwith ''what?''
```

108   S. Dolan et al.

4.2 Signal Handling and Asynchronous Effects

Even with the scoped masking combinators, it is difficult and unpleasant to write code that correctly manipulates resources in the presence of asynchronous exceptions. For this reason, many systems choose instead to poll for cancellation requests, instead of being interrupted with one. That is, instead of a `Sys.Break` exception being raised, the programmer manually and regularly checks a mutable boolean `cancellation_flag`, which is asynchronously set to `true` when the user presses `Ctrl-C` (This check may be combined with other system facilities: one common choice is that cancellation is checked at all I/O operations, since the program must handle failures there anyway).

On Unix-like systems, it is possible to implement this behaviour using a *signal handler*, which is a callback invoked when a signal is raised (e.g. by the user pressing `Ctrl-C`). In OCaml, these can be installed using the function `Sys.set_signal`. In fact, the behaviour of the previously-mentioned `Sys.catch_break` is implemented by installing a signal handler that raises `Sys.Break`:

```
set_signal sigint (Signal_handle (fun _ → raise Break))
```

Synchronous cancellation can be implemented using a signal handler that sets a cancellation flag:

```
let cancellation_flag = ref false
let is_cancelled () = !cancellation_flag
let () =
  set_signal sigint (Signal_handle (fun _ →
    cancellation_flag := true))
```

By removing the possibly of cancellation except at designated points, the imperative parts of the system become safer and easier to write. However, as Marlow et al. [22] note, for the purely functional parts of the system asynchronous cancellation is both necessary and just as safe as synchronous: necessary, because inspecting the mutable cancellation state breaks referential transparency, and safe, because purely functional code holds no resources and pure computations can be abandoned without issue.

In order to call a pure function from imperative code while maintaining prompt cancellation, we need to switch from synchronous (polling) cancellation to asynchronous cancellation and back, by providing a combinator:

```
async_cancellable : (unit → α) → (unit → α option)
```

Normally, `async_cancellable f` returns `Some (f ())`. However, the computation `f` may be cancelled asynchronously, causing `async_cancellable f` to return `None`, ensuring that asynchronous cancellation does not affect the caller.

Our first attempt at such a mechanism looks like:

```
let sync_handler = Signal_handle (fun _ →
  cancellation_flag := true)
let async_handler = Signal_handle (fun _ →
  raise Break)
let async_cancellable f =
```

```
mask (fun () →
  match
    set_signal sigint async_handler;
    let result = unmask f in
    set_signal sigint sync_handler;
    result
  with
  | x → Some x
  | exception Break → None)
```

This code is tricky, due to its delicate mutation of global state. It is very similar to the code we saw earlier using set_mask and clear_mask, and even has the same bug: it leaves the wrong signal handler in place if f raises an exception.

As before, scoped combinators make such code easier to get right (or, more accurately, harder to get wrong). To this end, we introduce *asynchronous effects*, which are effects that can be performed asynchronously, just as asynchronous exceptions can be raised asynchronously. By treating Break as an asynchronous effect, we can mix synchronous and asynchronous cancellation reliably.

For synchronous cancellation, we handle the Break effect by setting a flag:

```
let cancellation_flag = ref false
let sync_cancellable f =
  mask (fun () →
    match unmask f with
    | result → result
    | effect Break k →
        cancellation_flag = true; continue k ())
```

Asynchronously-cancellable code can be implemented by handling the Break effect and discarding the continuation. Since effect handlers delimit the continuation, the asynchrony is limited to the specified function.

```
let async_cancellable f =
  mask (fun () →
    match unmask f with
    | result → Some result
    | effect Break k → None)
```

Instead of having a single global callback as the current signal handler, asynchronous effects allow handlers to delimit their scope and nest correctly.

4.3   Managing Multiple Computations with Asynchronous Effects

Unlike signal handlers, asynchronous effects get an explicit representation of the computation they interrupted by way of the continuation k. While signal handlers can only resume the computation or abandon it (by raising an exception), effect handlers have other options available. For instance, a scheduler which maintains a collection of tasks can switch to another task when handling an asynchronous effect, just as the scheduler in Fig. 1 does for the synchronous Yield effect. Using asynchronous effects the cooperative scheduler of Fig. 1 can be made preemptive, by asking the operating system to provide a periodic timer signal (using e.g. the Unix `timer_create` API), and adding a new clause to the scheduler:

```
| effect TimerTick k → enqueue (continue k); run_next ()
```

4.4 Asynchronous I/O Notifications

Operating systems provide several different I/O interfaces. The simplest is the direct-style *blocking I/O*, in which the program calls operating-system functions which do not return until the operation completes. This allows a straightforward style of programming in which the sequence of I/O operations matches the flow of the code. We aim to support this style of programming using alternative operating system interfaces that allow multiple I/O operations to be overlapped.

In Sect. 3.3, we saw one way of accomplishing this with effects, by using multiplexing mechanisms like `select`, `poll`, etc., which block until one of several file descriptors is ready. An alternative is *asynchronous I/O*, in which multiple operations are submitted to the operating system, which overlaps their execution. However, applications written using asynchronous I/O tend to have complex control flow which does not clearly explain the logic being implemented, due to the complexity of handling the operating system's asynchronous notifications of I/O completion.

We propose effects and handlers as a means of writing direct-style I/O code, but using the asynchronous operating system interfaces. We introduce two new effect operations: `Delayed`, which describes an operation that has begun and will complete later, and `Completed`, which describes its eventual completion. Both of these take an integer parameter, which identifies the particular operation.

Potentially long-running operations like `read` perform the `Delayed` effect, indicating that the operation has been submitted to the operating system but has not yet completed. Later, upon receipt of an operating-system completion notification, the asynchronous effect `Completed` is performed.

Using this mechanism, support for asynchronous completions can be added to the scheduler of Fig. 1 by adding clauses for the `Delayed` and `Completed` effects, where `ongoing_io` is an initially empty hash table:

```
| effect (Delayed id) k →
  Hashtbl.add ongoing_io id k
| effect (Completed id) k →
  let k' = Hashtbl.find ongoing_io id in
  Hashtbl.remove ongoing_io id;
  enqueue (fun () → continue k ());
  continue k' ()
```

In this sample, the continuation k of the `Delayed` effect is the continuation of the code performing the I/O operation, which instead of being immediately invoked is stored in a hash table until it can be invoked without blocking.

The continuation k of the `Completed` effect is the continuation of whichever fiber was running when the I/O completed. This scheduler chooses to preempt that fiber in favour of the fiber that performed the I/O. Equally, the scheduler could give priority to the running fiber, by swapping k and k' in the last lines.

5   Results

So far we have presented what we believe are compelling applications of effect handlers for elegant system programming. However, none of that would matter if the resultant programs were unacceptably slower compared to extant solutions. Hence, in this section, we evaluate the performance of a web server built with effect handlers against existing production-quality web servers.

We have implemented an effect-based asynchronous I/O library, aeio [2], that exposes a direct-style API to the clients. At its core, aeio uses the main loop engine from the Lwt library using the libev[2] event loop (using *epoll* in our experiments). For the OCaml web server, we use httpaf, which is a high performance, memory efficient, and scalable web server that uses the Async library [24] (also using *epoll* as its I/O system call). We then extended httpaf and implemented an effect handler based backend using aeio. The configurations we use for the evaluation are:

- **Effect:** Effect-based version which uses httpaf with aeio on the Multi-core OCaml compiler. The Multicore OCaml compiler was forked off vanilla OCaml version 4.02.2.
- **Async:** Vanilla OCaml version 4.03.0, using httpaf + Async 113.33.03.
- **Go:** Go 1.6.3 version of the benchmark using net/http package.

For comparison, all three configurations were constrained to only one core (using the GOMAXPROCS variable in the case of Go).

The evaluations were done on a 3 GHz Intel Core i7 with 16 GB of main memory running 64-bit Ubuntu 16.10. The client workload was generated by the wrk2[3] program. Each wrk2 run uses a fixed number of client connections that issues requests at a constant rate, and measures request latency and throughput.

Figure 2 shows the latency profiles for 1 min runs under two different configurations. At 1k connections and 10k requests per second, the effect implementation performs marginally better than Async. Go performs the best with all requests satisfied within 27 ms. The average request latency of effect configuration is 2.127 ms over 587969 requests. Under this configuration, the observed throughput is between 9780 and 9800 requests per second in all of the configurations.

At high loads, the performance degrades substantially in every configuration, but it is worse in the OCaml implementations. The average latency for satisfying a client request increases to 333.40 ms in the effect case, while it is 139 ms in async and 107.25 ms in Go. While Go achieved 17389 requests per second, Async and effect implementations achieved only 16761 and 15440 requests per

---

[2] http://software.schmorp.de/pkg/libev.html.
[3] https://github.com/giltene/wrk2.

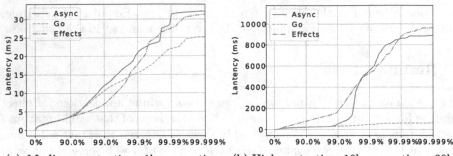

(a) Medium contention: 1k connections, (b) High contention: 10k connections, 30k
10k requests/sec   requests/sec

Fig. 2. Latency profile of client requests

second, respectively. This indicates that there is room for optimisations. Multicore OCaml has a new garbage collector, which has not been tuned to the extent
of vanilla OCaml and Go. We strongly suspect that garbage collector optimi-
sation and tuning would lead to performance improvements. Importantly, the
tail latencies of both OCaml implementations (the vanilla Async and our effect-
based server) were comparable in both configurations, indicating that there is no
significant performance degradation from our switch to using the effects model
presented in this paper.

6   Related Work

Implementations of Effect Handlers. Since their inception, several implementations of algebraic effect handlers have appeared, many of which are implemented
as libraries in existing programming languages [5,15–18,30,36]. There are several other implementations that like Multicore OCaml provide language level
support for effect handlers:

- Eff [4] is the first programming language designed with effect handlers in
  mind. It is a strict language with Hindley-Milner type inference similar in
  spirit to ML. It includes a novel feature for supporting fresh generation of
  effects in order to support effects such as ML-style higher-order state. Eff
  compiles to a free monad embedding in OCaml [29].
- Frank [21] is a programming language with effect handlers but no separate
  notion of function: a function is but a special case of a handler. Frank has a
  bidirectional type and effect system with a novel form of effect polymorphism.
  Furthermore, the handlers in Frank are so-called *shallow handlers*, which do
  not implicitly wrap themselves around the continuation, thereby allowing
  nonuniform interpretations of operations.
- Koka is a functional web-oriented programming language which has recently
  been enriched with effect handlers [20]. It has a type-and-effect system which

is based on row polymorphism. Koka uses a novel type-and-effect driven selective CPS compilation scheme for implementing handlers on managed platforms such as .NET and JavaScript.
- Links [7] is a single source, statically typed language with effect tracking for multi-tier web programming. Links supports effect handlers on both the client and the server. The server side implementation is based on a generalised abstract CEK machine [12], while the client side implementation is based on a CPS translation [13]. Links also has a prototype compiler for the server side with effect handlers based on the Multicore OCaml compiler [14].

A common theme for the above implementations is that their handlers are *multi-shot* handlers which permit multiple invocations of continuations.

Asynchronous IO. Many systems seek to combine the simplicity of direct-style, blocking I/O with the performance gains of allowing independent operations to complete in parallel. Indeed, the blocking I/O interfaces of most operating systems are designed in this way, by descheduling a process that requests a slow operation and running another process until the operation completes. However, operating system mechanisms rely on hardware context switching. The high overheads of such mechanisms lead to a desire for lightweight concurrent tasks integrated into programming languages.

The Erlang system [33] is a good example, capable of managing large numbers of lightweight processes with an integrated scheduler, and multiplexing their I/O onto operating system interfaces like `select`, `poll`, etc. More recently, the work by Syme et al. [32] adding `async`/`await` to F# allows the programmer to specify which operations should be completed asynchronously, implemented by compiling functions which use `async` differently from those that do not. The work by Marlow et al. on Concurrent Haskell [23] also supports large numbers of concurrent threads with multiplexed I/O, while allowing possibly-blocking operating system services to be used without blocking the entire system via the mechanism of *safe foreign calls*. Leijen [19] describes an implementation of a full-fledged async-await library implemented using effect handlers in Koka including cancellation and timeout. Koka compiles to JavaScript, whose concurrency model is cooperative. In particular, there are no asynchronous interrupts in JavaScript and Koka does not need the associated machinery to safely handle them.

Resource Handling with Control Operators. Programming languages supporting systems programming and exceptions generally support some variant of the `try-finally` idiom, often with syntactic support. For example, `try{...}finally{...}` in Java, `using` statements in C#, destructors and RAII in C++, or `defer` in Go.

Languages with more powerful control operators require correspondingly more powerful constructs for safe resource handling. The Common LISP condition system allows conditions (similar to effects) to be handled by abandoning the computation with an error, restarting it or ignoring the error and continuing, but does not allow the continuation to be captured as a value. It supports the unwind-protect form to ensure that cleanup code is run no matter how a block is exited. See Pitman [26] for an analysis of the condition system's design.

Scheme supports general nonlinear continuations [1], which present difficulties when handling inherently linear resources. Many Scheme implementations provide a primitive dynamic-wind [11], which generalises the try-finally idiom by taking some setup and cleanup code to be run not just once but every time control passes in and out of a specified block of code. However, this comes with its own caveats: the naive approach of using dynamic-wind to open and close a file will close and reopen the file every time a computation is paused and resumed, which is not safe in general as the file may not still exist at the second opening. One-shot (linear) continuations have also been proposed for Scheme [6].

Support for truly asynchronous interrupts is more rare, partially due to the difficulty of programming in their presence. The Unix signalling mechanism is an important example, but its reliance on global mutable state makes programming difficult (see Sect. 4.2). Marlow et al. [22] present a more composable design for asynchronous exceptions in Haskell. Our approach can be viewed as the extension of the Haskell approach to effects as well as exceptions.

7   Conclusion

Multicore OCaml provides effect handlers as a means to abstract concurrency. In this paper, we have described and demonstrated the utility of effect handlers in concurrent system oriented programming. We have developed a direct-style asynchronous I/O with effect handlers [2]. Using this library, we built a highly concurrent and scalable web server. Our evaluation shows that this implementation retains a comparative performance with the current state of the art in vanilla OCaml, but that OCaml has some room for improvement *vs* direct-style multicore concurrency in Go.

Rather than providing the full generality of effect handlers with nonlinear continuations, our design provides effect handlers with linear continuations. This design admits a particularly efficient implementation. Furthermore, linear continuations interplay more smoothly with system resources. Our implementation of asynchronous effects also provides an elegant solution to handling problematic corner cases in typical operating system interfaces, such as reliable signal handling and efficiently implementing quirky system call interfaces while exposing a simple, portable interface to the developer.

Acknowledgements. Daniel Hillerström was supported by EPSRC grant CDT in Pervasive Parallelism (EP/L01503X/1). K.C. Sivaramakrishnan was supported by a Research Fellowship from the Royal Commission for the Exhibition of 1851.

References

1. Abelson, H., Dybvig, R.K., Haynes, C.T., Rozas, G.J., Adams, N., Friedman, D.P., Kohlbecker, E., Steele, G., Bartley, D.H., Halstead, R., et al.: Revised(5) report on the algorithmic language Scheme. High. Order Symbolic Comput. **11**(1), 7–105 (1998)
2. Aeio: An asynchronous, effect-based I/O library (2017). https://github.com/kayceesrk/ocaml-aeio. Accessed 05 May 2017
3. Barroso, L., Marty, M., Patterson, D., Ranganathan, P.: Attack of the killer microseconds. Commun. ACM **60**(4), 48–54 (2017). https://doi.org/10.1145/3015146
4. Bauer, A., Pretnar, M.: Programming with algebraic effects and handlers. J. Logical Algebraic Methods Program. **84**(1), 108–123 (2015)
5. Brady, E.: Programming and reasoning with algebraic effects and dependent types. In: Proceedings of the 18th ACM SIGPLAN International Conference on Functional Programming, ICFP 2013, pp. 133–144. ACM, New York (2013). https://doi.org/10.1145/2500365.2500581
6. Bruggeman, C., Waddell, O., Dybvig, R.K.: Representing control in the presence of one-shot continuations. In: Fischer, C.N. (ed.) Proceedings of the ACM SIGPLAN 1996 Conference on Programming Language Design and Implementation (PLDI), 21–24 May 1996, pp. 99–107. ACM, Philadephia (1996)
7. Cooper, E., Lindley, S., Wadler, P., Yallop, J.: Links: web programming without tiers. In: de Boer, F.S., Bonsangue, M.M., Graf, S., de Roever, W.-P. (eds.) FMCO 2006. LNCS, vol. 4709, pp. 266–296. Springer, Heidelberg (2007). https://doi.org/10.1007/978-3-540-74792-5_12
8. Dolan, S., White, L., Madhavapeddy, A.: Multicore OCaml. In: OCaml Workshop (2014)
9. Dolan, S., White, L., Sivaramakrishnan, K.C., Yallop, J., Madhavapeddy, A.: Effective concurrency through Algebraic Effects. In: OCaml Workshop (2015)
10. Forster, Y., Kammar, O., Lindley, S., Pretnar, M.: On the expressive power of user-defined effects: effect handlers, monadic reflection, delimited control. Proceedings of ACM on Programming Languages, vol. 1(ICFP), pp. 13:1–13:29, August 2017. https://doi.org/10.1145/3110257
11. Friedman, D.P., Haynes, C.T.: Constraining control. In: Proceedings of the 12th ACM SIGACT-SIGPLAN Symposium on Principles of Programming Languages, POPL 1985, pp. 245–254. ACM, New York (1985). https://doi.org/10.1145/318593.318654
12. Hillerström, D., Lindley, S.: Liberating effects with rows and handlers. In: Proceedings of the 1st International Workshop on Type-Driven Development, TyDe 2016, pp. 15–27. ACM, New York (2016). https://doi.org/10.1145/2976022.2976033
13. Hillerström, D., Lindley, S., Atkey, R., Sivaramakrishnan, K.C.: Continuation passing style for effect handlers. In: Miller, D. (ed.) 2nd International Conference on Formal Structures for Computation and Deduction (FSCD 2017). In: Leibniz International Proceedings in Informatics (LIPIcs), vol. 84, pp. 18:1–18:19. Schloss Dagstuhl-Leibniz-Zentrum fuer Informatik, Dagstuhl (2017). http://drops.dagstuhl.de/opus/volltexte/2017/7739
14. Hillerström, D., Lindley, S., Sivaramakrishnan, K.C.: Compiling links effect handlers to the OCaml backend. In: ML Workshop (2016)

15. Kammar, O., Lindley, S., Oury, N.: Handlers in action. In: Proceedings of the 18th ACM SIGPLAN International Conference on Functional Programming, ICFP 2013, pp. 145–158. ACM, New York (2013). https://doi.org/10.1145/2500365.2500590

16. Kiselyov, O., Ishii, H.: Freer Monads, more extensible effects. In: Proceedings of the 2015 ACM SIGPLAN Symposium on Haskell, Haskell 2015, pp. 94–105. ACM, New York (2015). https://doi.org/10.1145/2804302.2804319

17. Kiselyov, O., Sabry, A., Swords, C.: Extensible effects: an alternative to monad transformers. In: Proceedings of the 2013 ACM SIGPLAN Symposium on Haskell, Haskell 2013, pp. 59–70. ACM, New York (2013). https://doi.org/10.1145/2503778.2503791

18. Kiselyov, O., Sivaramakrishnan, K.C.: Eff directly in OCaml. In: ML Workshop (2016)

19. Leijen, D.: Structured asynchrony with algebraic effects. In: Proceedings of the 2nd ACM SIGPLAN International Workshop on Type-Driven Development, TyDe 2017, pp. 16–29. ACM, New York (2017). https://doi.org/10.1145/3122975.3122977

20. Leijen, D.: Type directed compilation of row-typed algebraic effects. In: Proceedings of the 44th ACM SIGPLAN Symposium on Principles of Programming Languages, POPL 2017, pp. 486–499. ACM, New York (2017). https://doi.org/10.1145/3009837.3009872

21. Lindley, S., McBride, C., McLaughlin, C.: Do be do be do. In: Proceedings of the 44th ACM SIGPLAN Symposium on Principles of Programming Languages, POPL 2017, pp. 500–514. ACM, New York (2017). https://doi.org/10.1145/3009837.3009897

22. Marlow, S., Jones, S.P., Moran, A., Reppy, J.: Asynchronous exceptions in Haskell. In: Proceedings of the ACM SIGPLAN 2001 Conference on Programming Language Design and Implementation, PLDI 2001, pp. 274–285. ACM, New York (2001). https://doi.org/10.1145/378795.378858

23. Marlow, S., Jones, S.P., Thaller, W.: Extending the Haskell foreign function interface with concurrency. In: Proceedings of the 2004 ACM SIGPLAN Workshop on Haskell, Haskell 2004, pp. 22–32. ACM, New York (2004). https://doi.org/10.1145/1017472.1017479

24. Minsky, Y., Madhavapeddy, A., Hickey, J.: Real World OCaml - Functional Programming for the Masses. O'Reilly (2013). http://shop.oreilly.com/product/0636920024743.do#tab_04_2

25. Moggi, E.: Notions of computation and monads. Inf. Comput. **93**(1), 55–92 (1991). https://doi.org/10.1016/0890-5401(91)90052-4

26. Pitman, K.M.: Condition handling in the Lisp language family. In: Romanovsky, A., Dony, C., Knudsen, J.L., Tripathi, A. (eds.) Advances in Exception Handling Techniques. LNCS, vol. 2022, pp. 39–59. Springer, Heidelberg (2001). https://doi.org/10.1007/3-540-45407-1_3

27. Plotkin, G., Power, J.: Adequacy for algebraic effects. In: Honsell, F., Miculan, M. (eds.) FoSSaCS 2001. LNCS, vol. 2030, pp. 1–24. Springer, Heidelberg (2001). https://doi.org/10.1007/3-540-45315-6_1

28. Plotkin, G.D., Pretnar, M.: Handling algebraic effects. Logical Methods Comput. Sci. **9**(4) (2013). https://doi.org/10.2168/LMCS-9(4:23)2013

29. Pretnar, M., Saleh, A.H., Faes, A., Schrijvers, T.: Efficient compilation of algebraic effects and handlers. Technical report CW 708, KU Leuven, Belgium, October 2017

30. Saleh, A.H., Schrijvers, T.: Efficient algebraic effect handlers for prolog. Theory Pract. Logic Program. **16**(5–6), 884–898 (2016)

31. Sivaramakrishnan, K.C., Harris, T., Marlow, S., Peyton Jones, S.: Composable scheduler activations for haskell. J. Funct. Program. **26**, e9 (2016)
32. Syme, D., Petricek, T., Lomov, D.: The F# asynchronous programming model. In: Rocha, R., Launchbury, J. (eds.) PADL 2011. LNCS, vol. 6539, pp. 175–189. Springer, Heidelberg (2011). https://doi.org/10.1007/978-3-642-18378-2_15
33. Virding, R., Wikström, C., Williams, M.: Concurrent Programming in ERLANG, 2nd edn. Prentice Hall International (UK) Ltd., Hertfordshire (1996)
34. Vouillon, J.: Lwt: a cooperative thread library. In: Proceedings of the 2008 ACM SIGPLAN Workshop on ML, ML 2008, pp. 3–12. ACM, New York (2008). https://doi.org/10.1145/1411304.1411307
35. Wadler, P.: The Essence of Functional Programming. In: Proceedings of the 19th ACM SIGPLAN-SIGACT Symposium on Principles of Programming Languages, POPL 1992, pp. 1–14. ACM, New York (1992). https://doi.org/10.1145/143165.143169
36. Wu, N., Schrijvers, T., Hinze, R.: Effect handlers in scope. In: Proceedings of the 2014 ACM SIGPLAN Symposium on Haskell, Haskell 2014, pp. 1–12. ACM, New York (2014). https://doi.org/10.1145/2633357.2633358

Automatically Introducing Tail Recursion in CakeML

Oskar Abrahamsson[✉] and Magnus O. Myreen

Chalmers University of Technology, Gothenburg, Sweden
{aboskar,myreen}@chalmers.se

Abstract. We describe and implement an optimizing compiler transformation which turns non–tail-recursive functions into equivalent tail-
recursive functions in an intermediate language of the CakeML compiler. CakeML is a strongly typed functional language based on Standard
ML with call-by-value semantics and a fully verified compiler. We inte-
grate our implementation into CakeML compiler, and provide a machine-
checked proof verifying that the observational semantics of programs is
preserved under the transformation. To the best of our knowledge, this is
the first fully verified implementation of this transformation in any modern compiler. Moreover, our verification efforts uncover surprising drawbacks in some of the verification techniques employed in several parts of
the CakeML compiler. We provide a work-around for these drawbacks,
and compare it to potential alternatives.

1 Introduction

Consider the following definition of a function length in an ML-like language:

```
fun length []      = 0
 | length (x :: xs) = length xs + 1
```

Regardless of what we choose as its name, the purpose of length should be immediately clear even to a novice functional programmer – it computes the length of
a list. However, this aesthetically pleasing style of programming comes at a price:
length is not *tail recursive*. Since tail-recursive functions will in general compile
to more space efficient and faster code, we give an equivalent tail-recursive definition of length:

```
fun length' []       acc = acc
 | length' (x :: xs) acc = length' xs (1 + acc)

fun length xs = length' xs 0
```

Functions written using tail calls enable compilers to perform a powerful
optimization called *tail call elimination*. In short, tail call elimination entails the
procedure of transforming tail-recursive functions into something which resembles a while loop. Since such a function has a recursive call to itself directly in tail

© Springer International Publishing AG, part of Springer Nature 2018
M. Wang and S. Owens (Eds.): TFP 2017, LNCS 10788, pp. 118–134, 2018.
https://doi.org/10.1007/978-3-319-89719-6_7

position (i.e. the 'last' position visited when evaluating an expression), no additional bookkeeping is required to store a return address for the recursive call – once the base case is reached, length' may simply return to the function which originally called it. Moreover, when a function performs a tail-call to itself, the locations in memory or registers in which the function arguments are stored can be reused for subsequent recursive calls. The benefits of the transformation are constant stack space usage as well as increased performance due to the reduced amount of bookkeeping.

CakeML. CakeML [4] is a strongly typed functional programming language with call-by-value semantics, based on Standard ML. It supports a large subset of the features present in Standard ML, including references, exceptions, modules and I/O. The CakeML compiler targets several common hardware architectures, including Intel x86, ARM, MIPS and RISC-V. The compiler is implemented in higher-order logic using the HOL4 proof assistant, and comes with a mechanically verified proof of correctness which guarantees that every valid CakeML source program is compiled into semantically compatible machine code.

Contributions. In this paper, we describe a fully verified implementation of an optimizing code transformation for functional programs, which automatically introduces tail recursion using accumulators. The implementation acts on an intermediate language in the fully verified CakeML compiler. Our contributions consist of extending the CakeML compiler with a self-contained phase performing the transformation, as well as a machine-checked proof of semantic preservation. To the best of our knowledge, ours is the first proven-correct implementation of this transformation existing in a compiler.

The verification approach taken in the internals of the CakeML compiler lacks a static type system, which restricts the kind of optimizations that we can verify using the existing approach. Although this approach has been sufficient to verify intricate optimizations that manages to put CakeML in the league of the OCaml and Poly/ML compilers on some benchmarks [7], some shortcomings are exposed when verifying the transformation presented in this paper. We give an account of these shortcomings and provide a workaround.

Notation. The notation we employ is as follows. ML code is typeset in sansserif with comments enclosed by (* ... *). With the exception of the examples in Sects. 1 and 2.1, all source code listings consist of function definitions and theorems in the higher-order logic of HOL4. The syntax of HOL closely resembles that of ML-style languages: constructors, keywords and function names are typeset in sans-serif. Variables are written in *italic*. Records are declared using

$$\text{my\_record} =$$
$$<| \text{ field1} := v1; \text{ field2} := v2; \ldots |>$$

and use . (dot) for projection and with for update. Logical equivalence is denoted by $\iff$. Implication and case-style pattern matching is denoted by $\Rightarrow$. All other logical connectives retain their usual meaning.

In addition to the above, we steer away from verbose abstract syntax when possible, instead employing a briefer mathematical notation for function applications and operations, e.g. $x + y$ for operations and $f\ x$ for the function f applied to the expression x.

2   Transforming Recursive Functions

In this section, we describe a code transformation for automatically transforming recursive functions into tail-recursive functions. Although the transformation is well-known [10], it is usually performed by the programmer at the source level. We start by providing an informal description of the transformation through a worked example in Sect. 2.1. The example is generalized to an algorithmic description of the steps of the transformation in Sect. 2.2.

2.1   Example: List Reversal

Consider the following naive implementation of a function which reverses a list:

```
fun  reverse  [] = []                          (* reverse_base *)
   | reverse (x :: xs) = reverse xs ++ [x]     (* reverse_rec  *)
```

The tail position in the recursive case of reverse contains a list append operation reverse xs ++ [x]. We will introduce a function reverse' such that for all xs and for all a, it holds that reverse' xs a = reverse xs ++ a. We proceed by specifying the recursive case:

```
fun  reverse ' (x :: xs) a = reverse (x :: xs) ++ a
```

Next, we substitute the definition of reverse_rec for the call on the right-hand side:

```
fun  reverse ' (x :: xs) a = (reverse xs ++ [x]) ++ a
```

We then utilize the associative property of (++), yielding

```
fun  reverse ' (x :: xs) a = reverse xs ++ ([x] ++ a)
```

Since the property reverse' xs a = reverse xs ++ a holds for all choices of a, we substitute reverse' xs [] for reverse xs by an inductive argument.

```
fun  reverse ' (x :: xs) a = reverse' xs [] ++ ([x] ++ a)
```

We apply the inductive argument once more, this time with [x] ++ a for a.

```
fun  reverse ' (x :: xs) a = reverse' xs (([x] ++ a) ++ [])
```

The same procedure is applied for the base case of reverse. Finally, we give the definition some touch-ups utilizing the definition of (++) and introduce an auxiliary function named so that reverse' may be used in place of the original reverse:

```
fun  reverse '  []          a = a
  |  reverse '  (x :: xs)  a = reverse '  xs  (x :: a)

fun  reverse  xs  =  reverse '  xs  []
```

2.2 Tail Recursion Using Accumulators

The transformation steps applied in Sect. 2.1 can be generalized to work with any operation in tail position, as long as it is associative and has an identity element. Let $+$ be some associative operator with identity 0, and let f be some recursive function. The key takeaway from the reverse-example is that whenever f has an operation

$$f\ x + a \tag{1}$$

in tail position, we can replace this operation by a tail call, by introducing a function f' satisfying

$$f'\ x\ a = f\ x + a. \tag{2}$$

The additional argument a to f' is commonly referred to as an *accumulator*, since it accumulates the partial sum of the result computed during the recursion. The production of such a function f' can be performed as follows, by rewriting the existing expression constituting the body of f:

1. For those expressions e in tail position that satisfy the form $e := f\ x + y$ for some x, y, replace e by $f'\ x\ (y + a)$, where f' is an unused function name.
2. For all other expressions e in tail position, replace them with the expression $e + a$.
3. Finally, rename f to f', and give it an additional argument pointed to by a. The name f is re-used for an auxiliary definition applying f' to the identity of $+$ by setting $f\ x = f'\ x\ 0$.

3   The BVI Language

The CakeML compiler recently received a new backend [8] which makes use of 12 intermediate languages (ILs) during compilation. The IL under consideration for our implementation is BVI (Bytecode-Value Intermediate language). BVI is a first-order functional language. Like all other ILs in the new CakeML compiler backend, its formal semantics is specified in terms of a functional big-step style [6] (see Sect. 4).

The abstract syntax of the BVI language is shown in Fig. 1. The type num corresponds to natural numbers, and op to one of the languages primitive operations, e.g. arithmetic, I/O, pointer dereference, etc. The meaning of the BVI expressions is as follows: Var i denotes a variable with de Bruijn-index i, Raise exc raises an exception exc, and Op op xs denotes a primitive operation op on the expressions xs. The expressions If and Let have their usual meaning. A Call expression is of the form Call $ticks$ $dest$ $args$ hdl, where $dest$ denotes an

```
exp =
    Var num                      (* de Bruijn-variable *)
  | If exp exp exp               (* If-then-else *)
  | Let (exp list) exp           (* Let-binding *)
  | Raise exp                    (* Raise exception *)
  | Tick exp                     (* Decrement semantics clock *)
  | Call num (num option)
       (exp list) (exp option)   (* Function call *)
  | Op op (exp list)             (* Primitive operation *)
```

Fig. 1. The abstract syntax of BVI.

address in the code table to the function being called, and *args* the function arguments. Optionally, the address *hdl* to a function acting as an exception handler is present. The *ticks* parameter to Call, and the Tick expression are related to the verification of semantics preservation under divergence, and are in practice no-ops.

3.1 Motivations for BVI

The transformation described in Sect. 2.2 is to be applied on BVI programs as a standalone stage in the CakeML compiler. At this stage of compilation, the input program has been divided into a list of functions stored in an immutable code store, which we call the *code table*. Each entry in the code table is a tuple of the form $((loc : num), (ar : num), (exp : exp))$, where *loc* is a (unique) address used to index into the table, *ar* defines the arity of the function, and *exp* the expression which constitutes its body. Our motivations for choosing BVI for this optimization are the following:

- The compiler stage which transforms a prior higher-level IL into BVI introduces new functions into the compiler code table, and keeps track of what function names are unused. This suits our purposes, since our transformation needs to introduce auxiliary definitions, i.e. using previously unused entries in the code table.
- BVI does not support closures. Determining equivalence between values in a language with closures is complicated, since closure values contain program expressions that would be changed by our transformation. Implementing the transformation in a first-order language greatly simplifies verification, as it enables us to use equality as equivalence between values before and after the transformation.

3.2 Tail Recursion in BVI

We will now give an outline of how the transformation from Sect. 2.2 is implemented in the BVI stage of the CakeML compiler. The transformation is restricted to expressions containing associative integer arithmetic and list append in tail position, for the reason that these can be detected at compile-time with relative ease.

1. We search the code table for entries (loc, ar, exp) in which exp contains at least one tail position in the shape of $f\ x \oplus y$, where f is the name of the function at address loc and $\oplus$ is any of the supported operations.
2. If the previous check succeeds, we create an expression exp_{OPT} by modifying the tail positions of exp:
   - Any expression $f\ x \oplus y$ is replaced by a function call $f'\ x\ (y \oplus a)$, where f' is a function at the next unused address loc' in the code table, and a is a variable pointing at a newly allocated argument of the function.
   - Any other expression y in tail position is replaced by $y \oplus a$.
3. Finally, the transformed expression exp_{OPT} is inserted into the code table as $(loc', ar + 1, exp_{\mathrm{OPT}})$, and an auxiliary expression exp_{AUX} is inserted as $(loc, ar, exp_{\mathrm{AUX}})$. This expression simply calls f' while appending the identity of $\oplus$ to the arguments it was called with.

The algorithm described above is simple enough that it is tempting to instantly proceed with verifying its correctness. First, however, we need to take into consideration the following limitations that are specific to our setting.

Order of Evaluation. Aside from introducing tail-recursion, the transformation described in this section will also change the order in which sub-expressions to the transformed expressions are evaluated. In our case, substituting $f'\ x\ y$ for $f\ x \oplus y$ implies that y is moved forward in the order of evaluation. To preserve the order in which observable side effects – such as I/O events – appear, we need to impose additional restrictions on expressions such as $f\ x \oplus y$. In fact, restricting the contents of the expression y is sufficient to preserve the semantics under the transformation.

Types of Expressions. As with all ILs in the CakeML compiler, the BVI language lacks static type information. However, the transformation described in this section involves the replacement of function base cases y with $y \oplus a$, where a is the accumulating variable. Although the type of a is known statically, the type of y is not, and proving semantics preservation comes with the obligation to show that the operation $\oplus$ is correctly applied.

Not only must we address the previously stated issues so that the implemented transformation is correct, but we must also ensure that it is done in such a way that correctness can be proven using the verification techniques employed in the CakeML compiler. In particular, our proofs must be w.r.t. the existing formal semantics of BVI, which is defined in the next section.

4   The BVI Semantics

Like all ILs in the CakeML compiler, the semantics of BVI is defined in a functional big-step style using an interpreter function [6] called evaluate. The interpreter evaluate (see Fig. 2) takes as input a list of expressions, an environment of concrete values, and a semantics state. The semantics state is the following record type. Here, refs is a mapping from an identifier to a concrete pointer, and global is a reference to a dynamic array used for storing global variables. The field ffi contains a state which tracks the calls made to the foreign function interface. Lastly, clock is a natural number used by the semantics to track divergence.

α state =
 <| refs : (num $\mapsto$ v ref);   (* pointers to ref:s *)
    clock : num;   (* the compiler clock *)
    global : (num option);   (* pointer to global variables *)
    code : ((num $\times$ exp) num_map); (* compiler code table *)
    ffi : (α ffi_state)   (* FFI state *)
 |>

For a list of expressions xs, an environment env and a semantics state s, the term evaluate (xs,env,s) reduces to a tuple (r,t) where t is a post-state, and r is one of two different outcomes:

1. If the evaluation succeeds for all expressions in xs the result r is Rval vs, where vs is a list of concrete values, each corresponding to an expression in xs.
2. Should the semantics get stuck (i.e. fail) for some expression in xs, the result r is Rerr e, where e is an error which originates from the first failing expression in xs. Such errors are are divided into two categories:
   (a) Rraise a, resulting from an expression which raises an exception. Here a is the result of evaluating exc in the BVI expression Raise exc.
   (b) Rabort e, where e is one of:
      i. Rtimeout_error, if the evaluation of some expression in xs diverged.
      ii. Rtype_error, if an expression was ill-typed, or we attempted to access an unbound variable.

The type inference algorithm used in the CakeML compiler comes with proof of soundness and completeness [9]. This means that the semantics of any program for which a type can be inferred is guaranteed to not get stuck with a Rtype_error. Since all ILs in the compiler lack static type information, this is the closest we will get to a guarantee that programs are well-typed in our theorems.

5   Analysis of Expressions

We will now outline a method to statically determine the suitability of BVI functions for transformation, taking into consideration the limitations listed in Sect. 3.2, and the language semantics from Sect. 4. In particular, the latter will be required to make informed decisions about the detection of the types of expression, since the absence of type errors in the semantics is the only such information at hand.

```
evaluate ([],env,s) = (Rval [],s)
evaluate (x::y::xs,env,s) =
case evaluate ([x],env,s) of
  (Rval v₁,s₁)  ⇒
    (case evaluate (y::xs,env,s₁) of
      (Rval vs,s₂)  ⇒  (Rval (hd v₁::vs),s₂)
      | (Rerr v₈,s₂)  ⇒  (Rerr v₈,s₂))
  | (Rerr v₁₀,s₁)  ⇒  (Rerr v₁₀,s₁)
evaluate ([Var n],env,s) =
if n < length env then (Rval [el n env],s)
else (Rerr (Rabort Rtype_error),s)
evaluate ([If x₁ x₂ x₃],env,s) =
case evaluate ([x₁],env,s) of
  (Rval vs,s₁)  ⇒
    if Boolv T = hd vs then evaluate ([x₂],env,s₁)
    else if Boolv F = hd vs then evaluate ([x₃],env,s₁)
    else (Rerr (Rabort Rtype_error),s₁)
  | (Rerr v₇,s₁)  ⇒  (Rerr v₇,s₁)
  ...
evaluate ([Op op xs],env,s) =
case evaluate (xs,env,s) of
  (Rval vs,s′)  ⇒
    (case do_app op (reverse vs) s′ of
      Rval (v₃,v₄)  ⇒  (Rval [v₃],v₄)
      | Rerr e  ⇒  (Rerr e,s′))
  | (Rerr v₁₀,s′)  ⇒  (Rerr v₁₀,s′)
evaluate ([Tick x],env,s) =
if s.clock = 0 then (Rerr (Rabort Rtimeout error),s)
else evaluate ([x],env,dec_clock 1 s)
```

Fig. 2. Some cases of the interpreter evaluate which defines the semantics of BVI.

Purity. Aside from exceptions, all sources of impurity in the BVI language stem from Op expressions (see Fig. 1). These include operations that perform allocations, access references, or give rise to I/O events. Hence, purity can be ensured by restricting the usage of such operations, and avoiding expressions that raise exceptions.

Types. The types of some BVI expressions can be determined statically under the assumption that their evaluation will not get stuck with a type error in the semantics (see Sect. 4):

- Constants, such as integer literals or the empty list nil.
- Primitive operations such as integer arithmetic and list append.

Additionally, it is sometimes possible to statically determine the type of variables, provided that they exist under primitive operations. By mimicking the order used by evaluate (see Fig. 2) when traversing expressions, it is possible to determine the type of variables under operations, as the semantics of a misapplied operation will always get stuck with a type error. Our implementation constructs a context of local type information, allowing the type of a variable to be accessed if it is encountered during later stages of analysis.

Order of Evaluation. The method of inferring types described herein relies on the fact that expressions do not get stuck with an error in the semantics. This turns out to be insufficient knowledge about an expression that is to be lifted into an accumulating argument as described in Sect. 3.2; any such expression is required to reduce to a concrete and well-typed value. We postpone discussing the reasons for this until Sect. 6. Instead, we note that the method described above can be extended to provide termination guarantees, as long as the restrictions are recursively applied to the sub-expressions of primitive operations, and variables are ensured to be bound (see Fig. 2).

Taking into account the restrictions described in this section, the implementation from Sect. 3.2 is modified to work in two passes. In its first pass, the procedure searches for suitable looking function definitions, and ensures that the relevant sub-expressions of the program are well-typed and/or have the required purity and termination properties. If this holds, the necessary details are passed along to a second pass which rewrites the expression following the original description of the implementation.

6   Semantics Preservation

In this section we outline the process of verifying the correctness of the BVI implementation described in Sect. 3. In our setting, correctness means the preservation of observational semantics.

Since our transformation works on the entire program code table – as opposed to lists of expressions – it does not fit well into any of the existing stages in the BVI phase of the compiler. We have therefore implemented it as a stand-alone stage. In addition to proving theorems which state that observational semantics are preserved when transforming single expressions, this also requires us to prove a higher-level semantics theorem, stating that the semantics of all expressions in the code table are preserved under the transformation.

Semantics of Programs. A BVI program is represented as a compiler code table together with a starting address (the program entry-point) and an initial state. Program semantics are described by the semantics function semantics (see Fig. 3) which is defined in terms of evaluate. Intuitively, the semantics function describes the behavior of a call to the address declared as the programs entry-point.

- If the semantics of the call gets stuck with an error that is not a timeout error (i.e. it does not diverge), then the evaluation got stuck with either a type error or an uncaught exception. Such programs receive semantics Fail.
- If the evaluation of the call terminates with a concrete value, the program semantics is Success.
- Otherwise, should the program diverge, the semantics is Diverge tr, where tr is the least upper bound of the traces of I/O events in the FFI states obtained when evaluating k steps in the semantics of the call, for all $k \in \mathbb{N}$ (see Sect. 4 and Fig. 3). Since the operational semantics is deterministic, tr can be viewed as the possibly infinite trace obtained from allowing the evaluation to continue indefinitely.

For an explanation of the semantics function in greater detail, see Owens, et al. [6].

```
semantics init_ffi code start =
  let es = [Call 0 (Some start) [] None] in
  if ∃ k e.
      fst (evaluate (es,[],initial_state init_ffi code k)) =
      Rerr e ∧ e ≠ Rabort Rtimeout_error
  then Fail
  else
    case some res.
      ∃ k s r outcome.
        evaluate (es,[],initial_state init_ffi code k) = (r,s) ∧
        (case (s.ffi.final_event,r) of
          (None,Rval v₉) ⇒ outcome = Success
        | (None,Rerr v₁₀) ⇒ F
        | (Some e,v₃) ⇒ outcome = FFI_outcome e) ∧
        res = Terminate outcome s.ffi.io_events
    of None ⇒
      Diverge
      (⋁ k.
        (snd (evaluate (es,[], initial_state init_ffi code k))).ffi.io_events)
    | Some res ⇒ res
```

Fig. 3. The semantics of BVI programs.

Preserving Program Semantics. Using the semantics definition, we state the following semantics preservation theorem for our program transformation called compile_prog. Since all ill-typed programs are eliminated at an earlier stage of compilation (see Sect. 4), we restrict our theorem to *valid* programs, i.e. those with non-Fail semantics.

Theorem 1. *The semantics of any valid BVI program is preserved under the transformation* compile_prog.

$$
\begin{array}{l}
\vdash \text{every (free\_locs } n \circ \text{fst) } prog \,\wedge \\
\quad \text{all\_distinct (map fst } prog) \,\wedge \\
\quad \text{snd (compile\_prog } n \; prog) = prog_2 \,\wedge \\
\quad \text{semantics } \textit{ffi } prog \; start \neq \text{Fail} \Rightarrow \\
\quad \text{semantics } \textit{ffi } prog \; start = \\
\quad \text{semantics } \textit{ffi } prog_2 \; start
\end{array}
$$

Here, all_distinct ensures that the locations used for lookups into the code table are unique, and free_locs n that there are free slots for auxiliary functions in the code table starting at location n. Since semantics is defined in terms of evaluate proof of Theorem 1 requires a support theorem stated in terms of expression semantics.

Semantics of Expressions. To aid the proof of Theorem 1, we state the following theorem about the preservation of expression semantics under the transformation implemented in Sect. 3.2.

Theorem 2. *The semantics of any BVI expression evaluated in an environment env_1 and a state s is preserved under the transformation* rewrite, *if the transformed expression is evaluated in an environment env_2 related to env_1 through* env_rel, *and a state with the code table c related to s.code through* code_rel, *and the context supplied to* scan_expr *is related to the environment env_1 through* ty_rel.

$$
\begin{array}{l}
\vdash \text{evaluate } (xs, env_1, s) = (r,t) \wedge \text{env\_rel } opt \; acc \; env_1 \; env_2 \,\wedge \\
\quad \text{code\_rel } s.\text{code } c \wedge \text{ty\_rel } env_1 \; ts \wedge (opt \Rightarrow \text{length } xs = 1) \,\wedge \\
\quad r \neq \text{Rerr (Rabort Rtype\_error)} \Rightarrow \\
\quad \text{evaluate } (xs, env_2, s \text{ with code} := c) = \\
\quad\quad (r,t \text{ with code} := c) \,\wedge \\
\quad\quad (opt \Rightarrow \\
\quad\quad\quad \forall \, op \; n \; exp \; arity. \\
\quad\quad\quad\quad \text{lookup } loc \; s.\text{code} = \text{Some } (arity, exp) \,\wedge \\
\quad\quad\quad\quad \text{optimized\_code } loc \; arity \; exp \; n \; c \; op \,\wedge \\
\quad\quad\quad\quad (\exists \, op' \; ty. \\
\quad\quad\quad\quad\quad \text{scan\_expr } ts \; loc \; [\text{hd } xs] = [(ty, \text{Some } op')] \,\wedge \\
\quad\quad\quad\quad\quad \text{ok\_type } op' \; ty \Rightarrow \\
\quad\quad\quad\quad\quad \text{let } x = \text{rewrite } (loc, n, op, acc, ts) \; (\text{hd } xs) \text{ in} \\
\quad\quad\quad\quad\quad\quad \text{evaluate } ([x], env_2, s \text{ with code} := c) = \\
\quad\quad\quad\quad\quad\quad \text{evaluate} \\
\quad\quad\quad\quad\quad\quad\quad ([\text{apply\_op } op \; (\text{hd } xs) \; (\text{Var } acc)], env_2, \\
\quad\quad\quad\quad\quad\quad\quad s \text{ with code} := c))
\end{array}
$$

The first few lines of Theorem 2 are quite common to any verification of an optimization in the CakeML compiler. First, we limit our treatment to expressions for which the semantics do not get stuck with a type error. Following this, the next few lines state that the semantics of the expressions xs is preserved in the transformed code table c.

The unusual part of Theorem 2 is the implication $opt \Rightarrow \ldots$ which states the behavior of any expression in xs subjected to the transformation. Before going into further detail we give a brief account of the functions and various relations used in the theorem.

- code_rel c_1 c_2 connects the code table locations of functions prior to transformation (in c_1) to those after transformation (in c_2).
- env_rel opt acc env_1 env_2 ensures that the environment env_1 is a prefix of env_2, and that the accumulator variable points to a well-typed concrete value in env_2 when evaluating a transformed expression.
- ty_rel connects the environment with the context used in analysis, and states that for any variable for which the type was detected during analysis, there exists some concrete value in the environment with the correct type.
- scan_expr ts loc exp performs the bulk of the work for the analysis phase. It takes a context ts of variable types and a code table address loc for detection of a recursive call, and returns the expression return type ty and the operation op' it finds in tail position.
- rewrite performs the accumulator transformation on a single expression utilizing the operation found by scan_expr.
- ok_type op ty ensures that the operation op is compatible with the return-type ty of the expression.
- Finally, additional guarantees about the locations and properties of transformed expressions are given by the predicate optimized_code.

The second part of Theorem 2 then states that any expression for which the analysis pass succeeds will be transformed by rewrite and have semantics equivalent to that of the operation under consideration applied to the original expression and the accumulator (cf. Sect. 2).

In most cases, the proof of Theorem 2 need only deal with recursively applied transformations. These follow trivially by the induction hypothesis. However, there are two cases that must receive special treatment.

Function Calls. As the transformation is applied to the entire code table, any function call may potentially end up in a transformed expression. In this case, the necessary information is available from code_rel and optimized_code, which provides explicit code table locations for transformed expressions, and ensure that the expressions in these locations have transformed by rewrite.

Operations. Operations in tail positions which satisfy the requirements detailed in Sects. 3.2 and 5 are to be replaced by equivalent tail calls. That is, operations $f\ x + y$ are to be replaced by $f'\ x\ (y + acc)$ for some accumulating variable acc and some function f' satisfying

$$f'\ x\ a = f\ x + a.$$

What is to be proven is that for such f' and some acc,

$$f\ x + y + acc \equiv f'\ x\ (y + acc)$$

where $\equiv$ denotes semantic equivalence under the interpreter evaluate. From associativity follows that

$$f\ x + y + acc \equiv f\ x + (y + acc)$$

and we would expect an inductive argument to yield that

$$f\ x + (y + acc) \equiv f'\ x\ (y + acc). \tag{3}$$

This is certainly true in a broader setting where the expression y is known to be well-typed, as the semantics for a well-typed pure expression will reduce to a well-typed concrete value. However, no such information is available in our setting. In particular, it would not be possible to prove that the semantics of the expression y would reduce to *any value at all* without the restrictions discussed in Sect. 5.

But why is a termination guarantee for the expression y needed? The culprit turns out to be the altered order in which the expressions $f\ x$ and y are evaluated post-transformation.

6.1   Order of Evaluation

As previously stated, our theorems are set up to disregard any expressions for which the semantics get stuck with a type error. In the case of transformed operations in Theorem 2, this guarantee entails that the semantics for the expression $f\ x + y$ (i.e. prior to the transformation taking place) will to not get stuck with a type error. However, this is not to be mistaken for a guarantee that $f\ x + y$ is correctly typed.

To see why this is true, consider the semantics for operations in the BVI semantics (see Fig. 2). The arguments to the operation are evaluated in a left-to-right fashion before being passed on to the auxiliary function do_app, which performs the actual operation on the concrete values. Although the function call $f\ x$ can not get stuck with a type error, it could, for instance, diverge. In that case the evaluation of the arguments $[f\ x;\ y]$ would get stuck at $f\ x$ with a timeout error. At this point we can deduce nothing about the expression y, as its semantics is completely overshadowed by the semantics of $f\ x$. In particular, the semantics of y could very well get stuck with a type error, in which case the semantics of $f'\ x\ y$ would get stuck with a type error, so that Eq. (3) fails to hold.

Conclusion. We conclude this section by noting that the above issues are not in any way unique to the CakeML compiler. Instead, they are a consequence of the decision to use a operational semantics as a means of enforcing the correctness of programs without including static type information.

7   Related Work

Burstall and Darlington [1] described a framework for transforming recursive functions into more efficient iterative counterparts by unfolding function definitions. Their approach is arguably more powerful than the one we employ. However, it relies on a user-guided procedure, and is thus not suitable for inclusion in a fully automatic optimizing compiler.

An early systematic account of the transformation described in this paper was given by Wadler [10], with the primary goal of eliminating quadratic list append usage. Wadler notes that the transformation may be applied to various associative operations on a variety of data structures. In our setting, detecting non-primitive operations that may be optimized by the transformation is difficult. Moreover, we would be required to prove that all detected operations satisfy the associative property.

Another transformation for introducing accumulators is presented in Kühnemann et al. [3]. Although not limited to lists in the same ways as Wadler [10], the transformation appears to be limited to unary functions. We are not aware of any compiler which implements this transformation.

Chitil [2] describes an improvement of the short-cut deforestation algorithm which, among other improvements, enables deforestation to act on list producers which consume their own result. It correctly handles the reverse example from Sect. 2.1, but is limited to functions on lists, and requires static type information. It is therefore not suitable for implementation in our setting. As with Kühnemann et al. [3], we are not aware of any compiler which implements it.

In [5], Liu and Stoller shows how to transform general recursion into iteration by exploiting associativity. Their algorithm is able to transform both linear and non-linear recursion into iteration, and handles mutual recursion. The transformations are carried out in an imperative language with while loop statements. In our case, neither non-linear nor mutual recursion is supported, and it is unclear if doing so would bring any real benefits (see Sect. 8). Moreover, these additional features would come at the price of increasingly complex proofs when verifying semantics preservation, as our IL of choice is functional, where loops are expressed as recursion.

8   Discussion

The implementation of the transformation we describe in this paper can be used to lift arbitrary pure expressions into accumulating arguments when performed in a statically typed language. Although CakeML is statically typed, the IL in which we perform the transformation is not, and we are subsequently unable to fully utilize the potential of the transformation, as the semantics of our IL provides weak guarantees for 'well-typed' expressions (see Sects. 4 through 6).

We present a partial solution to these issues by means of an analysis pass which statically detects the type of most variables whenever they are used together with arithmetic, a relation on the integers, or list append. As long as their first appearance is not in tail position, they can be lifted into the accumulator. Moreover, we can track the types of variables to some extent, as long as there is not too much indirection.

An alternative approach to ours is to provide static type information. This can be done either by annotating expressions, or even introduce an entire type system for the BVI language. While this may appear attractive at first, any gains would be offset by a significant increase in effort: since end-to-end verification is employed in the CakeML compiler, all ILs prior to BVI would have to receive type systems, and preservation of types proven for all existing transformations. Introducing type annotations would lead to similar overhead.

Instead, we claim that our approach constitutes a sufficiently effective compromise. All analysis is local to the IL in which the transformation is performed, and does not disturb prior stages of compilation. In addition, it is hard to imagine sensible programs that *should* be optimized by the implementation, but cannot because of too much indirection.

Benefits and Drawbacks. Any recursive function which is transformed into a tail-recursive equivalent will no longer allocate additional stack frames when placing recursive calls to itself. As a consequence, functions that only call themselves during execution will have their stack space consumption bounded by a constant factor. In addition to reduced memory usage, these functions will see an increase in performance, as the allocation of new stack frames is a time-consuming process.

Rewriting recursive functions using accumulators is unlikely to introduce any shortcomings not already present in the transformed functions. However, an increase in the degree to which a compiler optimizes programs will lead to increased compile times. In our particular case, static analysis is as expensive as rewriting, implying an increase in compile times regardless if expressions were successfully rewritten or not.

In addition, the transformation presented in this work raises some interesting questions with regards to the notion of semantical compatibility. Although no notion of memory exists in the upper layers of the CakeML backend, the lowest levels take into account various limitations of the target architectures, including memory consumption. Hence, although semantics at the BVI level are *equivalent* under the transformation, it might 'repair' programs which would previously run out of stack space at the machine code level. At the time of writing, we have not proved that this optimization leads to less "out-of-memory" errors.

Future Work. Although we have settled on an approach which successfully estimates the types of some BVI expressions, there are likely more alternatives that we are simply unaware of. We could also extend the method currently employ, although sufficient extensions would simply tend towards a dynamic type system that can be called upon statically, and the trade-off when compared against providing static type information may just not be worth it.

Our transformation currently supports functions that perform linear recursion. Supporting non-linear recursion is possible, but requires more sophisticated machinery for purity-checking. In particular, we need to ensure the purity of entire functions, and provide proof that this knowledge can be applied locally in an expression.

Like Standard ML, CakeML is somewhat restricted in its support for mutual recursion. Hence, it is unclear if the effort required to support mutual recursion is worth it. However, our implementation could be strengthened to support operations in tail position containing recursive calls to *any* functions in scope. This could be achieved by threading the BVI code table through the functions performing the transformation while keeping track of which function definitions that have previously received an accumulating definition.

9   Summary

We have described an implementation of an optimizing compiler transformation acting on an IL in the CakeML compiler. The transformation introduces tail recursion in certain recursive functions on the integers and lists, and is verified to preserve the observational semantics of programs that are transformed. To the best of our knowledge, this is the first fully verified implementation of this transformation in any modern compiler.

Acknowledgments. This work was carried out as the first author's M.Sc. project, under the supervision of the second author. The authors would like to extend their thanks to the Lars Pareto scholarship for sponsoring the travel to the TFP symposium. We are grateful for comments on drafts of this text provided by Johannes Åman Pohjola. Finally, we thank the anonymous reviewers for their helpful feedback.

References

1. Burstall, R.M., Darlington, J.: A transformation system for developing recursive programs. J. ACM (JACM) **24**(1), 44–67 (1977)
2. Chitil, O.: Type-inference based short cut deforestation (nearly) without inlining. In: Koopman, P., Clack, C. (eds.) IFL 1999. LNCS, vol. 1868, pp. 19–35. Springer, Heidelberg (2000). https://doi.org/10.1007/10722298_2
3. Kühnemann, A., Glück, R., Kakehi, K.: Relating accumulative and non-accumulative functional programs. In: Middeldorp, A. (ed.) RTA 2001. LNCS, vol. 2051, pp. 154–168. Springer, Heidelberg (2001). https://doi.org/10.1007/3-540-45127-7_13
4. Kumar, R., Myreen, M., Norrish, M., Owens, S.: CakeML: a verified implementation of ML. In: Principles of Programming Languages (POPL). ACM (2014)
5. Liu, Y.A., Stoller, S.D.: From recursion to iteration: what are the optimizations? ACM Sigplan Not. **34**(11), 73–82 (1999)
6. Owens, S., Myreen, M.O., Kumar, R., Tan, Y.K.: Functional big-step semantics. In: Thiemann, P. (ed.) ESOP 2016. LNCS, vol. 9632, pp. 589–615. Springer, Heidelberg (2016). https://doi.org/10.1007/978-3-662-49498-1_23
7. Owens, S., Norrish, M., Kumar, R., Myreen, M.O., Tan, Y.K.: Verifying efficient function calls in CakeML. In: International Conference on Functional Programming (ICFP). ACM Press, September 2017

8. Tan, Y.K., Myreen, M.O., Kumar, R., Fox, A., Owens, S., Norrish, M.: A new verified compiler backend for CakeML. In: International Conference on Functional Programming (ICFP). ACM Press (2016)
9. Tan, Y.K., Owens, S., Kumar, R.: A verified type system for CakeML. In: Implementation and Application of Functional Programming Languages (IFL), p. 7. ACM (2015)
10. Wadler, P.: The concatenate vanishes. Note, University of Glasgow (1987)

The CakeML Compiler Explorer
Tracking Intermediate Representations
in a Verified Compiler

Rikard Hjort$^{(\boxtimes)}$, Jakob Holmgren , and Christian Persson

Chalmers University of Technology, Gothenburg, Sweden
{hjortr,jakhol,chrp}@student.chalmers.se

Abstract. It is difficult to understand how a compiler's different phases transform a program, especially if the only way to do so is by studying the compiler's source code. We have constructed a tool for the verified CakeML compiler which allows programmers to step through its phases, much like stepping through a program with a debugger. In particular, we allow a programmer to see how a piece of source code is represented in intermediate languages during compilation, and how pieces of intermediate code at different phases relate to each other. It is our hope that this feature will let the developers of CakeML more easily identify compiler optimizations, and that it will make it easier for new developers to quickly gain an intuition for the compiler.

1 Introduction

A compiler can be quite an opaque piece of software. It may generate large amounts of intermediate code, structured for other compiler phases—not humans—to work with. Ideally, a developer would want to be able to understand each transformation of the compiler, not only by reading the compiler code but also by observing the intermediate representations and see how they relate to each other. If a debugger is available, the developer might observe the compiler transformations by stepping through them and seeing them happen. Or, they might print intermediate representations and trace the expressions of interest between the representations. Both these processes may be tedious and error-prone. This project suggests a new way of observing a compiler's behavior and making it more accessible to study. The approach is specifically tailored to the structure of a functional compiler, written as a pure function from source program to machine words. By regarding each compilation phase as performing a reduction of this function, we can relate each expression in each intermediate language to the expressions it gets reduced into, letting a developer see how their program is translated, step by step, or several steps at once, without them needing to trace expressions manually.

For this project, we use the CakeML compiler, which is written as a pure function. CakeML is a verified implementation of a subset of Standard ML [11]. The compiler backend is proven to preserve the semantics of the input program at

M. Wang and S. Owens (Eds.): TFP 2017, LNCS 10788, pp. 135–148, 2018.
https://doi.org/10.1007/978-3-319-89719-6_8

every step, from source code to machine-code [13]. This is achieved by developing each compiler phase alongside a theorem of its correctness [10]. The CakeML project also stands out as an interesting project in the research field of verified compilation, as it is the first such compiler to be bootstrapped, meaning it can create an executable of itself, complete with a proof of the correctness of the executable [13]. The CakeML compiler is particularly well suited for this project as it uses many small, well-defined compilation steps, making the compilation process relatively easy to follow.

We turn to an example of the mentioned opaqueness of compilers. Consider a simple program in CakeML:

```
val x = 3 + 5;
```

Even when we take such a simple program and run it through the frontend and first phase of the CakeML compiler, the result is this quite complex looking intermediate representation[1]:

```
Prompt NONE [
    Dlet 1 (Mat (App (Op Opapp) [
        App (Op Opapp) [Var_global 155; Lit (IntLit 3)];
        Lit (IntLit 5)
    ]) [(Pvar "x", Pcon NONE [Var_local "x"])])
]
```

Four compiler phases later, the compiled program has grown even more complex, and has become hard for humans to read:

```
(Let (Seq (Extend_global 1) (Handle (Seq (Seq (Let (Let (App (Op Opapp) [App (Op Opapp)
[Var_global 155; Lit (IntLit 3)]; Lit (IntLit 5)]) (Pcon (SOME 0) [Var_local 89])) (Let
(App (El 0) [Var_local 89]) (Seq (App (Init_global_var 231) [Var_local 90]) (Pcon (SOME 0)
[])))) (Pcon (SOME 0) [])) (Pcon (SOME 0) [])) [(Pvar 89, Pcon (SOME 0) [Var_local 89])]))
(If (App (Tag_eq 0 0) [Var_local 89]) (Pcon (SOME 0) []) (Var_local 89)))
```

The developers of CakeML have expressed a desire for a tool which could output intermediate representations like the ones shown above, with some extended capabilities. The tool would let the user choose two or more intermediate representations to view and allow clicking any part of the source code or intermediate code, which would lead to the corresponding expressions in the other representations to be highlighted. For example, clicking 5 in the source code above would highlight Lit (IntLit 5) in the intermediate representations. By allowing this sort of click highlighting, it is believed that it will be easier for the developers to find possible optimizations to add to the compiler, and also that it will be easier to teach new developers how the compiler works.

The purpose of this paper is to describe how we have made the necessary extensions to the CakeML compiler to allow tracking expressions as they move through phases and to show a proof-of-concept implementation of an interactive

---

[1] This intermediate representation is abbreviated. The actual representation contains a large number of pre-defined functions which can be referenced as global variables. For instance, here + has been compiled to Var_global 155.

tool of the sort the CakeML developers have asked for. The key contributions we make are the following:

- We introduce a recursive datatype, described in Sect. 2, called *trace*, which is used to encode ancestry of expressions as they move through the compiler. We then annotate every expression in each intermediate language of the compiler with a trace. By comparing the traces of two expressions, we can decide whether they are related or not, i.e., if one was created from the other during compilation. The datatype also encodes source position so that, by looking at an expression in an intermediate state, one can determine in which exact position or positions in the source code the expression originated.
- We introduce three new intermediate languages which are used to compile the program state after each phase into JSON format [6], complete with the encoded ancestry information. In Sect. 3.1 we describe how we turn intermediate compiler representations into a standard format. From there, we can transform the program into a simple structure, described in Sect. 3.2, which can then easily be output in the desired format, in our case JSON.
- We present a simple web interface in Sect. 3.4 which displays the state of the compiler after different phases and which can highlight expressions in different states which are related.

Our solution is designed to work with a pure functional compiler.[2] The solution is constrained by the proved correctness of the compiler: since the compiler proof demonstrates that the semantics of the input program are preserved at each compiler phase, any large structural changes to the compilation process may cause significant trouble in updating intermediate proofs. We shall cope with these constraints by introducing only small changes to the intermediate languages that will carry the information we need to relate expressions to each other, and then breaking free of the standard compilation process, introducing an orthogonal translation process, which will make outputting the necessary information a simple matter, and release this process from the burden of correctness proofs. We have not attempted to prove any properties of this process at this stage, such as maintaining the well-formedness of traces, but have instead focused on interfering as little as possible with the existing proofs of compiler correctness.

2   Tracking Expressions

The first problem we have solved is that of encoding which expressions in different compiler states are related. Our solution is a recursive datatype which we use to annotate expressions in the compiler's intermediate languages. We call this datatype "trace", or `tra` in the compiler code. Trace values serve as a fingerprint of origin—all expressions with the same trace are of shared origin, and traces

---

[2] Thus, even though we will sometimes use the term "state", it has nothing to do with program state, but rather with various stages of evaluation.

can be built upon to create new, unique fingerprints, while still preserving information of origin. At a later point, we use this information to display ancestry of expressions through a graphical interface, as will be described in Sect. 3.4.

Annotating expressions means simply adding a trace as the first argument to expression constructors.[3] For example, the expression constructor

Let (string option) exp exp

becomes

Let tra (string option) exp exp.

With this approach, each expression carries information of its origin that can be read at any point of compilation, while not requiring any more updates to the correctness proofs than ignoring the tra parameter. The trace will not be carried along to the machine-code output of the compiler and is thus alleviated of the burden of having to be proved to preserve semantics. We will show how the trace is read together with the rest of the program after each compiler phase in Sect. 3, through a separate translation process. This allows us to limit the total changes to the compiler itself to adding the traces and logic for building them.

Figure 1 shows the definition of the tra datatype. It is a recursive type with two non-recursive constructors, SourceLoc and None. SourceLoc is the constructor used to terminate recursion. We use None only for the particular purpose of turning traces off when they are not needed, e.g., when compiling normally. There are also two recursive constructors, ▷ and Union. Here, ▷ is an infix constructor which can also be written as Cons in prefix form.

Using this datatype, we start by giving every expression in the source AST a unique trace. We do this by taking the source position and encoding it in a

```
tra =
    SourceLoc num num num num
  | (▷) tra num
  | Union tra tra
  | None
```

Fig. 1. tra datatype. Used for encoding the path any one expression has taken through the compiler, where ▷ encodes expressions being split and Union encodes expressions being merged.

---

[3] The decision to use this form of annotation rather than adding a new annotating constructor to each language was made in collaboration with the core CakeML development team. The reasoning is that new mutually recursive datatypes would complicate the compiler semantics and therefore the existing proofs, especially since we do not wish to force the annotation to always be present. Furthermore, modifying each constructor should be a one-off modification, since adding more metadata to the compilation process in the future could be accomplished by modifying the tra datatype.

SourceLoc. In the example program val x = 3 + 5; the source position of the partially applied function expression 3 + is from line 1, character 9, up to and including line 1, character 11, and the initial trace for this expression would be:

$$\text{SourceLoc 1 9 1 11.} \tag{1}$$

For all compiler phases following the initial one, traces are only allowed to grow or remain unchanged, never shrink. Traces grow either by extending a trace with ▷ or by joining two traces together with Union. This gives us three possible ways the trace of an expression may be altered as the expression is transformed during a compiler phase. Each correlates to a way that the expression itself may change, as this is exactly what the trace is supposed to inform us about.

The first case is when a compiler phase transforms an expression into exactly one new expression. In this case, the trace will get passed on as is to the new expression, which informs us no splitting or merging of expressions has taken place.

The second case is when an expression is turned into more than one new expression by a compiler phase. For example, when transforming an expression such as (fn x => foo x (x + 5)) 4 into foo 4 (4 + 5) by inlining, we want to be able to show that both instances of 4 in the result originate from the same 4 before the transformation. When this happens, the ▷ constructor is used to decorate the old trace with new numbers, starting from 1, producing as many new unique traces as necessary. For example, if the expression carrying the trace shown in (1) gets split into two expressions at a compiler phase, we would invent two new traces, the only difference between them being the outermost number:

$$\begin{aligned}
(\text{SourceLoc 1 9 1 11}\,) \rhd 1 \\
(\text{SourceLoc 1 9 1 11}\,) \rhd 2.
\end{aligned} \tag{2}$$

The third and last case to consider is when expressions get merged. Merging is rarer than splitting but is to be expected when performing certain optimizations, e.g., constant folding. If for example, the expressions 3 + and 5 are folded into one expression, 8, we would need some way of knowing that 8 originates in both 3 + and 5. Using the Union constructor, we can join the traces of 3 + and 5 together, to obtain the following trace:

$$\begin{aligned}
&\text{Union} \\
&(\text{SourceLoc 1 9 1 11}\,) \\
&(\text{SourceLoc 1 9 1 13}\,).
\end{aligned} \tag{3}$$

To state the rules of growing expressions formally: whenever a compiler function sees two or more expressions being defined on the right-hand side of the definition, and only one on the left, we use ▷ to split the trace into several new traces which we attach to the new expressions. Conversely, whenever two or more expressions appear on the left-hand side of a definition, and only one appears on the right, we apply Union to merge the traces.

To decode ancestry from traces, i.e., to determine whether one expression is the descendant of another, we look at the traces of both expressions. An expression e_1 with the trace t_1 is the ancestor of another expression e_2 with the trace t_2, if and only if t_2 can be derived from t_1. For a familiar metaphor, we can view the traces as binary trees, where a $\triangleright$ constructor is a node with a numerical value and a left child, Union is a node with no value and two children, and SourceLoc a leaf node with a four-tuple of numerical values. Then we can say with certainty that e_2 was derived from e_1 if and only if t_1 is a subtree of t_2. Note that when t_1 and t_2 are identical, this approach considers e_1 and e_2 to be ancestors of each other, and we must make use of the order of their respective intermediate languages to determine which is the ancestor, and which is the descendant.

The following pseudocode function determines whether a trace is the exact same trace as another, by checking that the traces have the exact same construction, including the same original source positions. Traces containing None are considered invalid for encoding ancestry, and using such a trace will always give the result False.

```
equals (SourceLoc a b c d) (SourceLoc a' b' c' d') =
    a == a' && b == b' && c == c' && d == d'

equals (t ▷ n)  (t' ▷ n') =
    n == n' && equals t t'

equals (Union t1 t2) (Union t1' t2') =
    equals t1 t1' && equals t2 t2'

equals _ _ = False
```

Using the above function, we can construct the following function that determines if one trace is the ancestor of another trace. It does not consider two equal traces to be ancestors of each other.

```
is_ancestor t (t' ▷ n) = equals t t' || is_ancestor t t'

is_ancestor t (Union t1 t2) =
    eqauls t t1
    || equals t t2
    || is_ancestor t t1
    || is_ancestor t t2

is_ancestor _ _ = False
```

This function deconstructs the second trace one step at a time, at each step checking for equality with the first trace. If the second trace is a SourceLoc, then the second trace cannot have been constructed from the first, and the result is False.

3   Presentation

Since the existing compiler implementation is a pure function, in which the intermediate representations have no memory of previous reductions, it is necessary that we add some information to intermediate expressions which maintains this memory. This is achieved in a relatively non-intrusive way through the trace datatype, as explained in the previous section. The remainder of the logic for relating expressions and presenting them then occurs without interfering with the regular compilation. To achieve this, we introduce three intermediate languages, and translations from intermediate compiler states to these languages.

This section covers our second contribution to the CakeML compiler, namely a sideways translation of sorts, that allows us to output every intermediate compiler state without further interference to the regular compilation. With this facility, we can translate the program into a semantics-free JSON representation. Each step of the translation serves a specific purpose. These are, respectively: to move to a more flexible intermediate language without formal semantics and thereby avoid the burden of correctness-proofs; to structure the representations, which cover all intermediate languages, into a simple yet comprehensive format; and to translate the structured representation into JSON. The final conversion to JSON is done in a thin, outer layer, and it is a simple exercise to implement other output formats with minimal changes. The JSON representation can then be used to present the intermediate states of regular compilation, as well as relating expressions in different intermediate representations to each other in the presentation, as will be explained in Sect. 3.4.

Figure 2 shows the flow through intermediate languages in the compiler. Each box contains the name of an intermediate language. Horizontal arrows represent

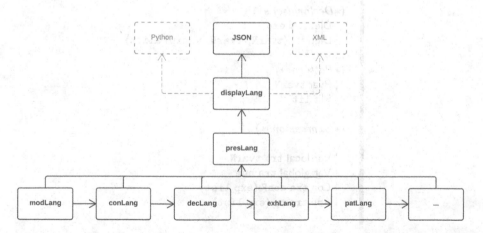

Fig. 2. Flow of a program through the modified compiler. Horizontal arrows indicate compilation with machine-code as the target, and vertical arrows represent translation with JSON as the target. Dashed boxes and arrows are possible but unimplemented alternative output formats.

regular compilation with machine-code as the target. Vertical arrows represent translation through our newly introduced intermediate languages, with JSON as the target.

3.1   Standard Presentation Format

The first step towards translating the intermediate representations into JSON is to move to a unified representation that captures the syntax of all existing intermediate languages. This representation has no formal semantics, since it will never be transformed into a runnable program, and therefore does not need correctness proofs. We want to create a single, unified type to represent the intermediate languages, so that we then can write a single function to translate this representation further, without having to take into account which intermediate language is being represented. Keeping with the spirit of the CakeML compiler, we make this first translation step from the existing intermediate languages small and almost trivial to implement, rather than translating directly into the smaller type which we will introduce in Sect. 3.2.

This first step is handled by the intermediate language PRESLANG. This language gathers every declaration, expression and pattern constructor of the existing intermediate languages into a single type. Figure 3 shows an abbreviation of the PRESLANG exp datatype. Since this type will only ever be presented, not evaluated, semantics and well-typedness of the program are pointless. Therefore,

```
exp =
   Prog (exp list)
   ...
(*Declarations*)
 | Dlet num exp
 | Dletrec ((tvarN, tvarN × exp) alist)
   ...
(*Patterns*)
 | Pvar tvarN
 | Plit lit
   ...
(*Expressions*)
   ...
 | Var_local tra tvarN
 | Var_global tra num
 | Con tra conF (exp list)
 | App tra op (exp list)
   ...
```

Fig. 3. PRESLANG exp datatype. In total, there are 37 constructors, and more are added as our explorer adds support for more intermediate languages. As can be seen, declarations, expressions, and patterns are not separated, since semantics and well-typedness are no longer a concern.

we do not need to separate declarations, expressions, and patterns, but can treat them as being of the same type, simplifying the language and further translation.

Here we also run into an issue we have not yet mentioned, that will limit our approach: most existing intermediate languages are represented by different types. Thus, a function from one intermediate language will not be able to accept an identical looking value from another intermediate language, since the types are incompatible. As the total number of intermediate languages are small and unlikely to change often, as are the types that represent each intermediate language, we cope with this issue by simply writing one function from each type to PRESLANG, which is quickly done.

3.2 Structuring Output

The language discussed in the previous section, PRESLANG, groups all declarations, expressions, and patterns from all intermediate language into a single expression type. This type constitutes a small transformation step from the existing intermediate languages but is unwieldy to work with. Thus, our next order of business is to condense PRESLANG expressions into a small and handy format to provide simplicity and consistency in the layer right before the final output layer.

We created the intermediate language DISPLAYLANG for this purpose. DISPLAYLANG has a single datatype, sExp, with three constructors:

sExp = Item (tra option) string (sExp list) | Tuple (sExp list) | List (sExp list).

An sExp expression may either be an Item with an optional trace, a name, and a list of expressions; a Tuple; or a List. The Tuple and List constructors correspond to the tuples and lists of expressions that intermediate language constructors take, while other source level primitives are expressed by a string representation in an Item constructor. This simple structure can capture the entirety of PRES-LANG, while having an easy to traverse tree structure, with strings and traces as the only type of information in the nodes. The addition of tuples and lists also makes for easy printing, as it is only a matter of printing the string contents of Item, surround lists with square brackets, tuples with parentheses, and proceed recursively. Here is an example of how an expression would be encoded in DISPLAYLANG. Imagine a constructor in PRESLANG, Foo ((num × num) list). For the final, printed output to show Foo [(1, 2)], the expression would be encoded in DISPLAYLANG as

Item NONE "Foo" [List [Tuple [Item NONE "1" [ ]; Item NONE "2" [ ]]]].

By going through this small language after PRESLANG, the final conversion to JSON becomes very thin, making it easy to add new output formats as needed. Perhaps even more importantly, this set-up provides consistency. The sExp datatype enforces a neat and predictable structure that can be directly translated into a JSON tree structure of named objects and lists, which can then be printed without knowledge of the underlying complexity in PRESLANG.

In the end, we translate DISPLAYLANG into JSON via a simple scheme: Item becomes an object with a **name** field containing the name of the original constructor, e.g., "Prog", its trace converted into a similar structure, and an array of objects in the field **args**; a Tuple is an object with a boolean **isTuple** flag and an array of **args**; and a List is simply turned into an array. The web interface presents this structure by printing it in flat form, with parentheses, and use the traces to associate parts of the presented strings with parts in other intermediate representations.

3.3 From de Bruijn Indices to Variable Names

Here we pause to note a special situation that occurs in translations into PRES-LANG. In PATLANG (the first intermediate language in the compiler chain which does not use pattern matches) and the two following intermediate languages, the compiler uses the notational scheme known as De Bruijn indexing [7]. This notation is convenient for compiler implementation and conducting proofs, as it removes possible naming conflicts in β-reduction. However, it is hard for humans to read, and we therefore replace the De Bruijn indices with standard variable names when presenting the compiler states.

As an example, consider the following expression in CakeML, which declares two mutually recursive local functions:

```
let
  fun f x = g x
  and g x = f x
in
  f 2
end
```

Figure 4 shows the result of calling pat_to_pres_exp, which converts a PATLANG expression to PRESLANG, on a simplified version of this expression in PATLANG. Look carefully at the occurrences of the numbers 0 and 1 before the conversion. The number 0 refers to either the input variable of the functions or to the first function, depending on context. Also, the first function is referred to as either 1 or 0, depending on context. In the result, each of the function definitions is converted to a tuple with three elements: (1) the function's name; (2) the name of its input variable; and (3) the function body. The first function is named "b" and the second "a". In all three occurrences of App, the two functions are referred to using the explicit names "a" and "b".[4]

---

[4] The names "b" and "a" are used instead of the source code names, "f" and "g". This is because in the conversion to PATLANG, the original names are discarded. It might be possible to reconstruct the original names using traces to determine the origin of each variable in PATLANG. However, this may not be feasible for the exact reason that De Bruijn indices are used, namely the risk of naming conflicts. A transformation may put two variables in the same namespace in a way that would cause a conflict if the original names were used. We therefore opted instead to create new variable names in a safe manner.

```
pat_to_pres_exp 0
  (Letrec t₁
    [App t₂ Opapp [Var_local t₃ 2;  Var_local t₄ 0];
     App t₅ Opapp [Var_local t₆ 1;  Var_local t₇ 0]]
    (App t₈ Opapp [Var_local t₉ 0;  Lit t₁₀ (IntLit 2)])) =
  Letrec t₁
    [("b","c",App t₂ (Patlang_op Opapp) [Var_local t₃ "a"; Var_local t₄ "c"]);
     ("a","c",App t₅ (Patlang_op Opapp) [Var_local t₆ "b"; Var_local t₇ "c"])]
    (App t₈ (Patlang_op Opapp) [Var_local t₉ "b"; Lit t₁₀ (IntLit 2)])
```

Fig. 4. Example of replacing De Bruijn indices with variable names. In the result, names have been assigned to the mutually recursive functions inside Letrec, and the functions are referred to using the explicit names "a" and "b".

Figure 5 shows two clauses of the function that performs this conversion. The number h is carried along at each call and counts how many bound variables are currently in scope, which is used to assign a unique variable name using a function, num_to_varn, that turns natural numbers into identifier strings.

```
pat_to_pres_exp h (Var_local t var_index) =
  Var_local t (num_to_varn (h − var_index − 1))
pat_to_pres_exp h (Fun t e) =
  Fun t (num_to_varn h) (pat_to_pres_exp (h + 1) e)
```

Fig. 5. Removing De Bruijn indexes in conversion to PRESLANG. The function pat_to_pres_exp takes a number, h, in addition to an expression. h is the number of currently bound variables in the scope. This value is used to compute fixed variable names from De Bruijn indices.

3.4 Web Application

Figure 6 shows our web application, with highlights on expressions corresponding to the literal 5 in our running example, val x = 3 + 5;. We print the languages horizontally and without pretty-printing for this proof-of-concept version of the web application. Around each object with a trace (corresponding to an Item in sExp), a <span> element is placed which we can use to highlight it. For each expression, we maintain information about its trace. When an expression in any language is clicked, its trace is sent via an event that is used to find and highlight all expressions in other intermediate representations it is related to.

```
val x = 3 + 5;

Compile

modLang
Prog [Prompt NONE [Dtype []]; Prompt NONE [Dtype []]; Prompt NONE [Dlet 1 (Mat (Fun "v3" (Mat (Var_local "v3") [(Pco

conLang
Prog [Prompt NONE []; Prompt NONE []; Prompt NONE [Dlet 1 (Mat (Fun "v3" (Mat (Var_local "v3") [(Pcon NONE [Pvar "v2'

decLang
Mat (Let NONE (Extend_global 0) (Handle (Let NONE (Pcon NONE []) (Pcon (SOME (0, TypeId (Short "option"))) []))) [(Pvi

exhLang
Mat (Let NONE (Extend_global 0) (Handle (Let NONE (Pcon (SOME 0). []) (Pcon (SOME 0) []))) [(Pvar "x", Pcon (SOME 0) ['

patLang
Let (SOME "a") (Seq (Extend_global 0) (Handle (Seq (Pcon (SOME 0) []) (Pcon (SOME 0) []))) [(Pvar "a", Pcon (SOME 0)
```

```
Dlet 1 (Mat (App (Op Opapp) [App (Op Opapp) [Var_global 155; Lit (IntLit 3)]; Lit (IntLit 3)]]) [(Pvar "x", Pcon NONE

)papp) [App (Op Opapp) [Var_global 155; Lit (IntLit 3)]; Lit (IntLit 5)]]) [(Pvar "x", Pcon NONE [Var_local "x"])]) [(

(Op Opapp) [Var_global 155; Lit (IntLit 3)]; Lit (IntLit 5)]]) (Pcon (SOME 0) [Var_local "cl"])) (Let (SOME "cm") (Ap
```

Fig. 6. Web application after compilation, and after clicking an expression. Three different intermediate languages are shown in the bottom image, with IntLit 5 clicked in the middle one. In reality, these expressions are not lined up, but may appear further apart. This figure shows them cropped together for convenience.

4 Related Work

What we have achieved is a way of presenting a compiler's inner workings by both showing intermediate representations, and how each expression in each intermediate representation relates to expressions before and after it. To the best of our knowledge, there is no other tool available that combines these features. We will briefly mention a selection of previous compiler explorers and their features. They have in common that they perform one of these feats—displaying intermediate states of compilation or relating sections of source code and target code—but not both.

The HERMIT tool is a plugin to the Glasgow Haskell Compiler, GHC, that lets Haskell programmers interact directly with the compilation of their source program [8]. By pausing compilation and allowing the programmer to view and interactively perform transformations on the GHC Core language AST, the programmer can find possible optimizations to their source program. HERMIT thus has powerful capabilities not present in the Compiler Explorer presented in this paper. HERMIT does not, however, implement something similar to our expression tracking, but relies on the programmer making manual edits and using version control of the edits to observe different outcomes.

There exists at least one tool for relating source code in C++, D, Rust, and Go code with corresponding assembly code, line by line [3]. In it, one can highlight the code in the source or the assembly, much the same way as one can in our interface described in Sect. 3.4. However, the tool does not show any intermediate states, and it is therefore not possible to follow the compiler's inner workings step by step via the tool.

There also exists several tools for outputting intermediate compiler states and information about them. Notably, there is an old, deprecated Compiler Explorer for CakeML [2], developed by Yong Kiam Tan. There is also an unparser for an educational compiler made by Sarkar et al. [12] which can pretty-print the compiler's intermediate states, and the LLVM Visualization Tool [4] which can display intermediate compiler states in a number of ways, such as with call hierarchies and control-flow graphs. What all these tools lack, however, is the possibility to relate sections of code in each intermediate language. One is presented only with the complete intermediate state, without any facilities to relate expressions in them. For anything but very simple programs, it becomes very difficult to follow the actual translation of sections of code and consequently what transformations the compiler actually performs at intermediate steps. On this basis, we believe our approach is viable and fills an important gap.

5   Summary

We have shown how to extend the pure functions of a verified compiler to be able to track expressions as they pass through compilation, and how this tracking information can be presented. To make it possible to track expressions, we introduce the `tra` datatype and show how its values can be built gradually to encode ancestry. To output this information, we introduce three new intermediate languages with the special purpose of translation that does not interfere with regular compilation but can still show the intermediate results of it. We have also developed a basic interactive interface for visualizing the tracking information.

The changes to the compiler are included in the master branch of the official CakeML repository [1] and our web application can be found in a separate repository [5].

Acknowledgements. The Compiler Explorer is a Bachelor's thesis project conducted by the authors of this paper at Chalmers University of Technology, and this paper summarizes the main points of the thesis [9]. We want to especially thank our supervisor, Magnus Myreen, for his great ideas and quick feedback. We also want to thank Ramana Kumar for patiently answering our questions in the CakeML and HOL IRC channels and the CakeML developer mailing lists, as well as the entire developer team behind CakeML, Magnus Myreen and Ramana Kumar included, for inviting us to contribute. Finally, we want to thank the anonymous reviewers for their constructive feedback.

References

1. CakeML: A Verified Implementation of ML. https://github.com/CakeML/cakeml. Accessed 15 Sept 2017
2. CakeML Compiler Explorer. https://cakeml.org/explorer.cgi. Accessed 4 Apr 2017
3. Compiler Explorer. https://github.com/mattgodbolt/compiler-explorer. Accessed 2 May 2017
4. LLVM Visualization Tool User Guide. https://llvm.org/svn/llvm-project/television/trunk/docs/UserGuide.html. Accessed 28 Apr 2017

5. Saser/compiler-explorer-react. https://github.com/Saser/compiler-explorer-react. Accessed 11 May 2017
6. Bray, T.: The javascript object notation (JSON) data interchange format (2014). https://tools.ietf.org/html/rfc7159.html
7. De Bruijn, N.G.: Lambda calculus notation with nameless dummies: a tool for automatic formula manipulation, with application to the Church-Rosser theorem. In: Indagationes Mathematicae (Proceedings), vol. 75, pp. 381–392. Elsevier (1972)
8. Farmer, A.: HERMIT: mechanized reasoning during compilation in the Glasgow Haskell Compiler. Ph.D. thesis, The University of Kansas, April 2015
9. Hjort, R., Holmgren, J., Persson, C.: The CakeML compiler explorer: visualizing how a verified compiler transforms expressions. Bachelor's thesis, Chalmers University of Technology, Department of Computer Science and Engineering, SE-412 96 Göteborg (2017). http://publications.lib.chalmers.se/records/fulltext/251308/251308.pdf
10. Kumar, R.: Self-compilation and self-verification, chap. 3, pp. 37–48, Technical report, UCAM-CL-TR-879, University of Cambridge, Computer Laboratory, February 2016. http://www.cl.cam.ac.uk/techreports/UCAM-CL-TR-879.pdf
11. Kumar, R., Myreen, M.O., Norrish, M., Owens, S.: CakeML: a verified implementation of ML. In: Symposium on Principles of Programming Languages [POPL]. ACM Press (2014)
12. Sarkar, D., Waddell, O., Dybvig, R.K.: A nanopass framework for compiler education. J. Funct. Program. 15(05), 653–667 (2005)
13. Tan, Y.K., Myreen, M.O., Kumar, R., Fox, A., Owens, S., Norrish, M.: A new verified compiler backend for CakeML. In: International Conference on Functional Programming [ICFP]. ACM Press, September 2016

Author Index

Printed in the United States
By Bookmasters